#DoBetter On Purpose Planning Reflection Journal:
A Guide to Self-Awareness

Copyright @2021 Joan Baucum-Robinson

All rights reserved.
No part of this book may be reproduced or transmitted
in any form or by any means
without written permission from the author.

Imprint: Independently published
Printed in the United States of America

Book Design & editing by Joan Baucum-Robinson
2nd Edition 2022

#DoBetter On Purpose Reflection Journal

A Guide to Self-Awareness

Joan Baucum-Robinson

#DoBetter On Purpose

This journal belongs to...

Self-Reflection is important for settling the acceptance of who we truly are. Assessing our feelings, thoughts, and actions daily. It is the basis for life changing awareness. Begin today by taking a deep dive into WHO you really are.

Maya Angelou Said:
"Do the best you can until you know better.
Then when you know better, do better."

So... #DoBetter On Purpose!

What is 1 thing you want to learn about yourself by using this Self-Reflection Journal?
Come back if you need time to think about it...

Further Reading
On Self-Awareness

Self-Awareness: The Hidden Driver of Success and Satisfaction
By: Travis Bradberry

The 7 Habits of Highly Effective People: Powerful Lessons in Personal Change
By: Stephen R. Covey, Jim Collins

Emotional Intelligence: Why It Can Matter More Than IQ
By: Daniel Goleman

Emotional Detox
7 Steps to Release Toxicity and Energize Joy
By: Sherianna Boyle

Control Your Mind and Master Your Feelings: This Book Includes -
Break Overthinking & Master Your Emotions
By: Eric Robertson

The Science of Emotional Resilience:
Find Balance and Strength, Become Unbreakable, and Overcome Adversity
By: Peter Hollins

Relational Intelligence:
The People Skills You Need for the Life of Purpose You Want
By: Dharius Daniels (Author), Judah Smith (Foreword)

©Joan Baucum-Robinson - On Purpose Reflection Journal

Meet Coach Joaniebop!

LIFE STRATEGIST & COACH

HELLO!
I LOVE TO EQUIP PEOPLE TO GROW INTO AUTHENTIC & PURPOSE-FILLED LEADERS. IT IS MY PRIVILEGE & HONOR TO WALK ALONGSIDE OTHERS USING MY PASSIONS AND GIFTINGS TO ACCELERATE CHANGE!
I RUN MY OWN BUSINESS CALLED ON PURPOSE PLANNING & CONSULTING, WORK AS AN INDUSTRIAL ENGINEER IN THE MARKETPLACE, AND ALSO A LEADERSHIP AND MINISTRY COACH FOR MY LOCAL CHURCH. I EVEN DABBLE IN THE RETAIL SPACE OF CUSTOM CREATIVE APPAREL AND JEWELRY WITH PURPOSE. GOD PLACED SO MANY TALENTS INSIDE OF ME, AND I INTEND TO LEAVE MY MARK HERE ON EARTH! THANK YOU FOR PICKING UP MY BOOK, I PRAY YOU ARE TRANSFORMED AND MADE NEW AS A RESULT!

©JOAN BAUCUM-ROBINSON - ON PURPOSE REFLECTION JOURNAL

My mission in life is not merely to survive, but to thrive; and to do so with some passion, some compassion, some humor, and some style.

MAYA ANGELOU

©Joan Baucum-Robinson - On Purpose Reflection Journal

#DoBetter On Purpose

A *guide* to using this journal

This Journal will give you prompts to challenge you to dig deep into your inner self to see **WHY** you do what you do.

It will focus on 3 main premises:

What is going **WELL** with you?

What is **NOT** going well with you?

And the *challenge*:

What will you **DECIDE** to do **DIFFERENT**?

Then continue to process your journaling on the Mind Dump page provided.

**I have provided enough prompts for 31 days each month because I don't want to number the months, or take away from when you picked this up. Please skip over the extra days and proceed forward, that way, you can stay on track with your progress.

Enjoy, Coach Joaniebop

©Joan Baucum-Robinson - On Purpose Reflection Journal

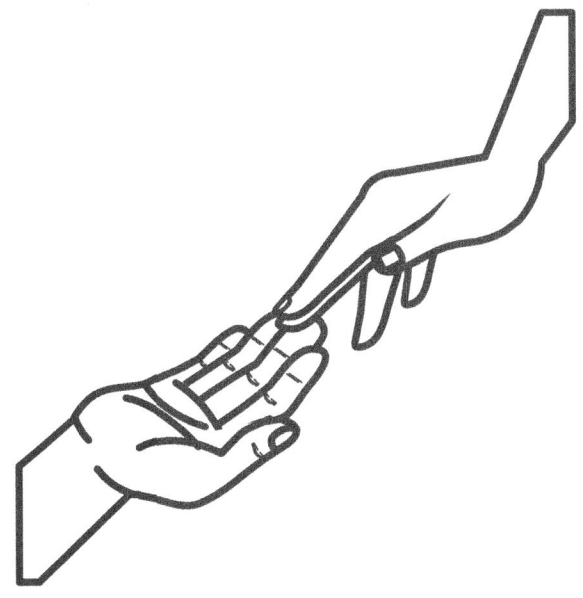

God has entrusted me with myself...

- EPICTETUS

Get out of **B.E.D.**

BLAME

EXCUSE

DENIAL

PUT ON YOUR **O.R.A.**

OWNERSHIP

RESPONSIBILITY

ACCOUNTABILITY

<u>Change is completely up to you</u>

WE ALLOW AND CREATE

THE CIRCUMSTANCES WE LIVE IN

So whether you think you can or cannot, is correct!

> As you start your journey, the first thing you should do is throw away that store-bought map and begin to draw your own.
>
> *Michael Dell*

Self Awareness Alignment

OUTLINE IN THESE CATEGORIES WHERE YOU WILL *FOCUS* YOUR SELF REFLECTION
WHAT THINGS WILL YOU KEEP IN THE FRONT OF YOUR MIND?

RELATIONSHIPS HEALTH

FINANCES LESIURE CAREER

SPIRITUALITY GROWTH

NOTES:
_____
_____

Intentional Habits
HOW WILL YOU BE INTENTIONAL?

REMEBER THESE IN YOUR DAILY REFLECTIONS

MORNING HABITS	MID-DAY HABITS	EVENING HABITS

What **DISCIPLINES** will you put into place?

What will be your **WINNING STRATEGIE**S to change what you see on a daily basis?

Try: Prayer/meditation, written reminders, and accountability partners...

Write below 2-3 things you are willing to commit to doing to change behaviors (Think it, Speak it, Write it, Work it)

▶

▶

▶

If you have Accountability **YOU HAVE OWNERSHIP!**

MY DAILY NEWSLETTER
SELF REFLECTION = SELF AWARENESS

WHAT'S 1 THING IN THE *OUTSIDE* WORLD THAT AFFECTED ME TODAY?

WHAT ARE 1-2 THINGS I AM CONTENT WITH IN MY LIFE TODAY? THANKFUL? GRATEFUL?

WHAT 3 THINGS WENT ON TODAY IN *MY WORLD* THAT STOOD OUT? WHAT MADE AN IMPACT?

WHAT DIDN'T GO WELL TODAY?

HOW DID I FEEL EMOTIONALLY? WRITE THEM OUT

HOW DID YOU FEEL PHYSICALLY? WHAT DO I NEED TO ADDRESS?
RESTRICTED BREATHING? ANXIOUSNESS? TENSION? GUT ISSUES? CHEST/BODY PAINS? WITHDRAWN?

ON THE OTHER HAND, WHAT DID GO WELL TODAY?

WHAT CONTRIBUTED TO THINGS GOING WELL?

READ WHAT YOU WROTE ABOVE…WHAT DO YOU THINK YOU NEED TO #DOBETTER ON PURPOSE TOMORROW?

MIND DUMP, PROCESS & UNRAVEL

If you have Accountability **YOU HAVE OWNERSHIP!**

MY DAILY NEWSLETTER
SELF REFLECTION = SELF AWARENESS

WHAT'S 1 THING IN THE *OUTSIDE* WORLD THAT AFFECTED ME TODAY?

WHAT ARE 1-2 THINGS I AM CONTENT WITH IN MY LIFE TODAY? THANKFUL? GRATEFUL?

WHAT 3 THINGS WENT ON TODAY IN *MY WORLD* THAT STOOD OUT? WHAT MADE AN IMPACT?

WHAT DIDN'T GO WELL TODAY?

HOW DID I FEEL EMOTIONALLY? WRITE THEM OUT

HOW DID YOU FEEL PHYSICALLY? WHAT DO I NEED TO ADDRESS?
RESTRICTED BREATHING? ANXIOUSNESS? TENSION? GUT ISSUES? CHEST/BODY PAINS? WITHDRAWN?

ON THE OTHER HAND, WHAT DID GO WELL TODAY?

WHAT CONTRIBUTED TO THINGS GOING WELL?

READ WHAT YOU WROTE ABOVE...WHAT DO YOU THINK YOU NEED TO #DoBetter ON PURPOSE TOMORROW?

MIND DUMP, PROCESS & UNRAVEL

If you have Accountability **YOU HAVE OWNERSHIP!**

MY DAILY NEWSLETTER
SELF REFLECTION = SELF AWARENESS

WHAT'S 1 THING IN THE *OUTSIDE* WORLD THAT AFFECTED ME TODAY?

WHAT ARE 1-2 THINGS I AM CONTENT WITH IN MY LIFE TODAY? THANKFUL? GRATEFUL?

WHAT 3 THINGS WENT ON TODAY IN *MY WORLD* THAT STOOD OUT? WHAT MADE AN IMPACT?

_____   _____   _____

WHAT DIDN'T GO WELL TODAY?

HOW DID I FEEL EMOTIONALLY? WRITE THEM OUT

HOW DID YOU FEEL PHYSICALLY? WHAT DO I NEED TO ADDRESS?
RESTRICTED BREATHING? ANXIOUSNESS? TENSION? GUT ISSUES? CHEST/BODY PAINS? WITHDRAWN?

ON THE OTHER HAND, WHAT DID GO WELL TODAY?

WHAT CONTRIBUTED TO THINGS GOING WELL?

READ WHAT YOU WROTE ABOVE...WHAT DO YOU THINK YOU NEED TO #DoBetter ON PURPOSE TOMORROW?

MIND DUMP, PROCESS & UNRAVEL

If you have Accountability **YOU HAVE OWNERSHIP!**

MY DAILY NEWSLETTER
SELF REFLECTION = SELF AWARENESS

WHAT'S 1 THING IN THE *OUTSIDE* WORLD THAT AFFECTED ME TODAY?

WHAT ARE 1-2 THINGS I AM CONTENT WITH IN MY LIFE TODAY? THANKFUL? GRATEFUL?

WHAT 3 THINGS WENT ON TODAY IN *MY WORLD* THAT STOOD OUT? WHAT MADE AN IMPACT?

WHAT DIDN'T GO WELL TODAY?

HOW DID I FEEL EMOTIONALLY? WRITE THEM OUT

HOW DID YOU FEEL PHYSICALLY? WHAT DO I NEED TO ADDRESS?
RESTRICTED BREATHING? ANXIOUSNESS? TENSION? GUT ISSUES? CHEST/BODY PAINS? WITHDRAWN?

ON THE OTHER HAND, WHAT DID GO WELL TODAY?

WHAT CONTRIBUTED TO THINGS GOING WELL?

READ WHAT YOU WROTE ABOVE...WHAT DO YOU THINK YOU NEED TO #DoBetter ON PURPOSE TOMORROW?

MIND DUMP, PROCESS & UNRAVEL

If you have Accountability **YOU HAVE OWNERSHIP!**

MY DAILY NEWSLETTER
SELF REFLECTION = SELF AWARENESS

WHAT'S 1 THING IN THE *OUTSIDE* WORLD THAT AFFECTED ME TODAY?

WHAT ARE 1-2 THINGS I AM CONTENT WITH IN MY LIFE TODAY? THANKFUL? GRATEFUL?

WHAT 3 THINGS WENT ON TODAY IN *MY WORLD* THAT STOOD OUT? WHAT MADE AN IMPACT?

_____   _____   _____

WHAT DIDN'T GO WELL TODAY?

HOW DID I FEEL EMOTIONALLY? WRITE THEM OUT

HOW DID YOU FEEL PHYSICALLY? WHAT DO I NEED TO ADDRESS?
RESTRICTED BREATHING? ANXIOUSNESS? TENSION? GUT ISSUES? CHEST/BODY PAINS? WITHDRAWN?

ON THE OTHER HAND, WHAT DID GO WELL TODAY?

WHAT CONTRIBUTED TO THINGS GOING WELL?

READ WHAT YOU WROTE ABOVE…WHAT DO YOU THINK YOU NEED TO #DoBetter ON PURPOSE TOMORROW?

MIND DUMP, PROCESS & UNRAVEL

If you have Accountability **YOU HAVE OWNERSHIP!**

MY DAILY NEWSLETTER
SELF REFLECTION = SELF AWARENESS

WHAT'S 1 THING IN THE *OUTSIDE* WORLD THAT AFFECTED ME TODAY?

WHAT ARE 1-2 THINGS I AM CONTENT WITH IN MY LIFE TODAY? THANKFUL? GRATEFUL?

WHAT 3 THINGS WENT ON TODAY IN *MY WORLD* THAT STOOD OUT? WHAT MADE AN IMPACT?

WHAT DIDN'T GO WELL TODAY?

HOW DID I FEEL EMOTIONALLY? WRITE THEM OUT

HOW DID YOU FEEL PHYSICALLY? WHAT DO I NEED TO ADDRESS?
RESTRICTED BREATHING? ANXIOUSNESS? TENSION? GUT ISSUES? CHEST/BODY PAINS? WITHDRAWN?

ON THE OTHER HAND, WHAT DID GO WELL TODAY?

WHAT CONTRIBUTED TO THINGS GOING WELL?

READ WHAT YOU WROTE ABOVE...WHAT DO YOU THINK YOU NEED TO #DoBetter ON PURPOSE TOMORROW?

MIND DUMP, PROCESS & UNRAVEL

If you have Accountability **YOU HAVE OWNERSHIP!**

MY DAILY NEWSLETTER
SELF REFLECTION = SELF AWARENESS

WHAT'S 1 THING IN THE *OUTSIDE* WORLD THAT AFFECTED ME TODAY?

WHAT ARE 1-2 THINGS I AM CONTENT WITH IN MY LIFE TODAY? THANKFUL? GRATEFUL?

WHAT 3 THINGS WENT ON TODAY IN *MY WORLD* THAT STOOD OUT? WHAT MADE AN IMPACT?

WHAT DIDN'T GO WELL TODAY?

HOW DID I FEEL EMOTIONALLY? WRITE THEM OUT

HOW DID YOU FEEL PHYSICALLY? WHAT DO I NEED TO ADDRESS?
RESTRICTED BREATHING? ANXIOUSNESS? TENSION? GUT ISSUES? CHEST/BODY PAINS? WITHDRAWN?

ON THE OTHER HAND, WHAT DID GO WELL TODAY?

WHAT CONTRIBUTED TO THINGS GOING WELL?

READ WHAT YOU WROTE ABOVE...WHAT DO YOU THINK YOU NEED TO #DoBetter ON PURPOSE TOMORROW?

MIND DUMP, PROCESS & UNRAVEL

If you have Accountability **YOU HAVE OWNERSHIP!**

MY DAILY NEWSLETTER
SELF REFLECTION = SELF AWARENESS

WHAT'S 1 THING IN THE *OUTSIDE* WORLD THAT AFFECTED ME TODAY?

WHAT ARE 1-2 THINGS I AM CONTENT WITH IN MY LIFE TODAY? THANKFUL? GRATEFUL?

WHAT 3 THINGS WENT ON TODAY IN *MY WORLD* THAT STOOD OUT? WHAT MADE AN IMPACT?

WHAT DIDN'T GO WELL TODAY?

HOW DID I FEEL EMOTIONALLY? WRITE THEM OUT

HOW DID YOU FEEL PHYSICALLY? WHAT DO I NEED TO ADDRESS?
RESTRICTED BREATHING? ANXIOUSNESS? TENSION? GUT ISSUES? CHEST/BODY PAINS? WITHDRAWN?

ON THE OTHER HAND, WHAT DID GO WELL TODAY?

WHAT CONTRIBUTED TO THINGS GOING WELL?

READ WHAT YOU WROTE ABOVE... WHAT DO YOU THINK YOU NEED TO #DoBetter ON PURPOSE TOMORROW?

MIND DUMP, PROCESS & UNRAVEL

If you have Accountability **YOU HAVE OWNERSHIP!**

MY DAILY NEWSLETTER
SELF REFLECTION = SELF AWARENESS

WHAT'S 1 THING IN THE *OUTSIDE* WORLD THAT AFFECTED ME TODAY?

WHAT ARE 1-2 THINGS I AM CONTENT WITH IN MY LIFE TODAY? THANKFUL? GRATEFUL?

WHAT 3 THINGS WENT ON TODAY IN *MY WORLD* THAT STOOD OUT? WHAT MADE AN IMPACT?

WHAT DIDN'T GO WELL TODAY?

HOW DID I FEEL EMOTIONALLY? WRITE THEM OUT

HOW DID YOU FEEL PHYSICALLY? WHAT DO I NEED TO ADDRESS?
RESTRICTED BREATHING? ANXIOUSNESS? TENSION? GUT ISSUES? CHEST/BODY PAINS? WITHDRAWN?

ON THE OTHER HAND, WHAT DID GO WELL TODAY?

WHAT CONTRIBUTED TO THINGS GOING WELL?

READ WHAT YOU WROTE ABOVE... WHAT DO YOU THINK YOU NEED TO #DoBetter ON PURPOSE TOMORROW?

MIND DUMP, PROCESS & UNRAVEL

If you have Accountability **YOU HAVE OWNERSHIP!**

MY DAILY NEWSLETTER
SELF REFLECTION = SELF AWARENESS

WHAT'S 1 THING IN THE *OUTSIDE* WORLD THAT AFFECTED ME TODAY?

WHAT ARE 1-2 THINGS I AM CONTENT WITH IN MY LIFE TODAY? THANKFUL? GRATEFUL?

WHAT 3 THINGS WENT ON TODAY IN *MY WORLD* THAT STOOD OUT? WHAT MADE AN IMPACT?

WHAT DIDN'T GO WELL TODAY?

HOW DID I FEEL EMOTIONALLY? WRITE THEM OUT

HOW DID YOU FEEL PHYSICALLY? WHAT DO I NEED TO ADDRESS?
RESTRICTED BREATHING? ANXIOUSNESS? TENSION? GUT ISSUES? CHEST/BODY PAINS? WITHDRAWN?

ON THE OTHER HAND, WHAT DID GO WELL TODAY?

WHAT CONTRIBUTED TO THINGS GOING WELL?

READ WHAT YOU WROTE ABOVE...WHAT DO YOU THINK YOU NEED TO #DoBetter ON PURPOSE TOMORROW?

MIND DUMP, PROCESS & UNRAVEL

If you have Accountability **YOU HAVE OWNERSHIP!**

MY DAILY NEWSLETTER
SELF REFLECTION = SELF AWARENESS

WHAT'S 1 THING IN THE *OUTSIDE* WORLD THAT AFFECTED ME TODAY?

WHAT ARE 1-2 THINGS I AM CONTENT WITH IN MY LIFE TODAY? THANKFUL? GRATEFUL?

WHAT 3 THINGS WENT ON TODAY IN *MY WORLD* THAT STOOD OUT? WHAT MADE AN IMPACT?

WHAT DIDN'T GO WELL TODAY?

HOW DID I FEEL EMOTIONALLY? WRITE THEM OUT

HOW DID YOU FEEL PHYSICALLY? WHAT DO I NEED TO ADDRESS?
RESTRICTED BREATHING? ANXIOUSNESS? TENSION? GUT ISSUES? CHEST/BODY PAINS? WITHDRAWN?

ON THE OTHER HAND, WHAT DID GO WELL TODAY?

WHAT CONTRIBUTED TO THINGS GOING WELL?

READ WHAT YOU WROTE ABOVE…WHAT DO YOU THINK YOU NEED TO #DoBetter ON PURPOSE TOMORROW?

MIND DUMP, PROCESS & UNRAVEL

If you have Accountability **YOU HAVE OWNERSHIP!**

MY DAILY NEWSLETTER
SELF REFLECTION = SELF AWARENESS

What's 1 thing in the *OUTSIDE* world that Affected me today?

What are 1-2 things I am content with in my life today? Thankful? Grateful?

What 3 things went on today in *My world* that stood out? What made an impact?

What didn't go well today?

How did I feel emotionally? Write them out

− +

How did you feel physically? What do I need to address? Restricted Breathing? Anxiousness? Tension? Gut issues? Chest/Body Pains? Withdrawn?

On the other hand, What did go well today?

What contributed to things going well?

Read what you wrote above...What do you think you need to #DoBetter on Purpose Tomorrow?

MIND DUMP, PROCESS & UNRAVEL

If you have Accountability **YOU HAVE OWNERSHIP!**

MY DAILY NEWSLETTER
SELF REFLECTION = SELF AWARENESS

WHAT'S 1 THING IN THE *OUTSIDE* WORLD THAT AFFECTED ME TODAY?

WHAT ARE 1-2 THINGS I AM CONTENT WITH IN MY LIFE TODAY? THANKFUL? GRATEFUL?

WHAT 3 THINGS WENT ON TODAY IN *MY WORLD* THAT STOOD OUT? WHAT MADE AN IMPACT?

WHAT DIDN'T GO WELL TODAY?

HOW DID I FEEL EMOTIONALLY? WRITE THEM OUT

HOW DID YOU FEEL PHYSICALLY? WHAT DO I NEED TO ADDRESS?
RESTRICTED BREATHING? ANXIOUSNESS? TENSION? GUT ISSUES? CHEST/BODY PAINS? WITHDRAWN?

ON THE OTHER HAND, WHAT DID GO WELL TODAY?

WHAT CONTRIBUTED TO THINGS GOING WELL?

READ WHAT YOU WROTE ABOVE...WHAT DO YOU THINK YOU NEED TO #DoBetter ON PURPOSE TOMORROW?

MIND DUMP, PROCESS & UNRAVEL

If you have Accountability **YOU HAVE OWNERSHIP!**

MY DAILY NEWSLETTER
SELF REFLECTION = SELF AWARENESS

WHAT'S 1 THING IN THE *OUTSIDE* WORLD THAT AFFECTED ME TODAY?

WHAT ARE 1-2 THINGS I AM CONTENT WITH IN MY LIFE TODAY? THANKFUL? GRATEFUL?

WHAT 3 THINGS WENT ON TODAY IN *MY WORLD* THAT STOOD OUT? WHAT MADE AN IMPACT?

WHAT DIDN'T GO WELL TODAY?

HOW DID I FEEL EMOTIONALLY? WRITE THEM OUT

HOW DID YOU FEEL PHYSICALLY? WHAT DO I NEED TO ADDRESS?
RESTRICTED BREATHING? ANXIOUSNESS? TENSION? GUT ISSUES? CHEST/BODY PAINS? WITHDRAWN?

ON THE OTHER HAND, WHAT DID GO WELL TODAY?

WHAT CONTRIBUTED TO THINGS GOING WELL?

READ WHAT YOU WROTE ABOVE... WHAT DO YOU THINK YOU NEED TO #DoBetter ON PURPOSE TOMORROW?

MIND DUMP, PROCESS & UNRAVEL

If you have Accountability **YOU HAVE OWNERSHIP!**

MY DAILY NEWSLETTER
SELF REFLECTION = SELF AWARENESS

WHAT'S 1 THING IN THE *OUTSIDE* WORLD THAT AFFECTED ME TODAY?

WHAT ARE 1-2 THINGS I AM CONTENT WITH IN MY LIFE TODAY? THANKFUL? GRATEFUL?

WHAT 3 THINGS WENT ON TODAY IN *MY WORLD* THAT STOOD OUT? WHAT MADE AN IMPACT?

_____   _____   _____

WHAT DIDN'T GO WELL TODAY?

HOW DID I FEEL EMOTIONALLY? WRITE THEM OUT

– ▬▬▬▬▬ +

HOW DID YOU FEEL PHYSICALLY? WHAT DO I NEED TO ADDRESS?
RESTRICTED BREATHING? ANXIOUSNESS? TENSION? GUT ISSUES? CHEST/BODY PAINS? WITHDRAWN?

ON THE OTHER HAND, WHAT DID GO WELL TODAY?

WHAT CONTRIBUTED TO THINGS GOING WELL?

READ WHAT YOU WROTE ABOVE…WHAT DO YOU THINK YOU NEED TO #DoBetter ON PURPOSE TOMORROW?

MIND DUMP, PROCESS & UNRAVEL

If you have Accountability **YOU HAVE OWNERSHIP!**

MY DAILY NEWSLETTER
SELF REFLECTION = SELF AWARENESS

WHAT'S 1 THING IN THE *OUTSIDE* WORLD THAT AFFECTED ME TODAY?

WHAT ARE 1-2 THINGS I AM CONTENT WITH IN MY LIFE TODAY? THANKFUL? GRATEFUL?

WHAT 3 THINGS WENT ON TODAY IN *MY WORLD* THAT STOOD OUT? WHAT MADE AN IMPACT?

WHAT DIDN'T GO WELL TODAY?

HOW DID I FEEL EMOTIONALLY? WRITE THEM OUT

HOW DID YOU FEEL PHYSICALLY? WHAT DO I NEED TO ADDRESS?
RESTRICTED BREATHING? ANXIOUSNESS? TENSION? GUT ISSUES? CHEST/BODY PAINS? WITHDRAWN?

ON THE OTHER HAND, WHAT DID GO WELL TODAY?

WHAT CONTRIBUTED TO THINGS GOING WELL?

READ WHAT YOU WROTE ABOVE...WHAT DO YOU THINK YOU NEED TO #DoBetter ON PURPOSE TOMORROW?

MIND DUMP, PROCESS & UNRAVEL

If you have Accountability **YOU HAVE OWNERSHIP!**

MY DAILY NEWSLETTER
SELF REFLECTION = SELF AWARENESS

WHAT'S 1 THING IN THE *OUTSIDE* WORLD THAT AFFECTED ME TODAY?

WHAT ARE 1-2 THINGS I AM CONTENT WITH IN MY LIFE TODAY? THANKFUL? GRATEFUL?

WHAT 3 THINGS WENT ON TODAY IN *MY WORLD* THAT STOOD OUT? WHAT MADE AN IMPACT?

WHAT DIDN'T GO WELL TODAY?

HOW DID I FEEL EMOTIONALLY? WRITE THEM OUT

HOW DID YOU FEEL PHYSICALLY? WHAT DO I NEED TO ADDRESS?
RESTRICTED BREATHING? ANXIOUSNESS? TENSION? GUT ISSUES? CHEST/BODY PAINS? WITHDRAWN?

ON THE OTHER HAND, WHAT DID GO WELL TODAY?

WHAT CONTRIBUTED TO THINGS GOING WELL?

READ WHAT YOU WROTE ABOVE...WHAT DO YOU THINK YOU NEED TO #DoBetter ON PURPOSE TOMORROW?

MIND DUMP, PROCESS & UNRAVEL

If you have Accountability **YOU HAVE OWNERSHIP!**

MY DAILY NEWSLETTER
SELF REFLECTION = SELF AWARENESS

WHAT'S 1 THING IN THE *OUTSIDE* WORLD THAT AFFECTED ME TODAY?

WHAT ARE 1-2 THINGS I AM CONTENT WITH IN MY LIFE TODAY? THANKFUL? GRATEFUL?

WHAT 3 THINGS WENT ON TODAY IN *MY WORLD* THAT STOOD OUT? WHAT MADE AN IMPACT?

WHAT DIDN'T GO WELL TODAY?

HOW DID I FEEL EMOTIONALLY? WRITE THEM OUT

HOW DID YOU FEEL PHYSICALLY? WHAT DO I NEED TO ADDRESS?
RESTRICTED BREATHING? ANXIOUSNESS? TENSION? GUT ISSUES? CHEST/BODY PAINS? WITHDRAWN?

ON THE OTHER HAND, WHAT DID GO WELL TODAY?

WHAT CONTRIBUTED TO THINGS GOING WELL?

READ WHAT YOU WROTE ABOVE...WHAT DO YOU THINK YOU NEED TO #DoBetter ON PURPOSE TOMORROW?

MIND DUMP, PROCESS & UNRAVEL

If you have Accountability **YOU HAVE OWNERSHIP!**

MY DAILY NEWSLETTER
SELF REFLECTION = SELF AWARENESS

WHAT'S 1 THING IN THE *OUTSIDE* WORLD THAT AFFECTED ME TODAY?

WHAT ARE 1-2 THINGS I AM CONTENT WITH IN MY LIFE TODAY? THANKFUL? GRATEFUL?

WHAT 3 THINGS WENT ON TODAY IN *MY WORLD* THAT STOOD OUT? WHAT MADE AN IMPACT?

WHAT DIDN'T GO WELL TODAY?

HOW DID I FEEL EMOTIONALLY? WRITE THEM OUT

HOW DID YOU FEEL PHYSICALLY? WHAT DO I NEED TO ADDRESS? RESTRICTED BREATHING? ANXIOUSNESS? TENSION? GUT ISSUES? CHEST/BODY PAINS? WITHDRAWN?

ON THE OTHER HAND, WHAT DID GO WELL TODAY?

WHAT CONTRIBUTED TO THINGS GOING WELL?

READ WHAT YOU WROTE ABOVE...WHAT DO YOU THINK YOU NEED TO #DoBetter ON PURPOSE TOMORROW?

MIND DUMP, PROCESS & UNRAVEL

If you have Accountability **YOU HAVE OWNERSHIP!**

MY DAILY NEWSLETTER
SELF REFLECTION = SELF AWARENESS

WHAT'S 1 THING IN THE *OUTSIDE* WORLD THAT AFFECTED ME TODAY?

WHAT ARE 1-2 THINGS I AM CONTENT WITH IN MY LIFE TODAY? THANKFUL? GRATEFUL?

WHAT 3 THINGS WENT ON TODAY IN *MY WORLD* THAT STOOD OUT? WHAT MADE AN IMPACT?

_____   _____   _____

WHAT DIDN'T GO WELL TODAY?

HOW DID I FEEL EMOTIONALLY? WRITE THEM OUT

HOW DID YOU FEEL PHYSICALLY? WHAT DO I NEED TO ADDRESS?
RESTRICTED BREATHING? ANXIOUSNESS? TENSION? GUT ISSUES? CHEST/BODY PAINS? WITHDRAWN?

ON THE OTHER HAND, WHAT DID GO WELL TODAY?

WHAT CONTRIBUTED TO THINGS GOING WELL?

READ WHAT YOU WROTE ABOVE... WHAT DO YOU THINK YOU NEED TO #DoBetter ON PURPOSE TOMORROW?

MIND DUMP, PROCESS & UNRAVEL

If you have Accountability **YOU HAVE OWNERSHIP!**

MY DAILY NEWSLETTER
SELF REFLECTION = SELF AWARENESS

WHAT'S 1 THING IN THE *OUTSIDE* WORLD THAT AFFECTED ME TODAY?

WHAT ARE 1-2 THINGS I AM CONTENT WITH IN MY LIFE TODAY? THANKFUL? GRATEFUL?

WHAT 3 THINGS WENT ON TODAY IN *MY WORLD* THAT STOOD OUT? WHAT MADE AN IMPACT?

WHAT DIDN'T GO WELL TODAY?

HOW DID I FEEL EMOTIONALLY? WRITE THEM OUT

HOW DID YOU FEEL PHYSICALLY? WHAT DO I NEED TO ADDRESS?
RESTRICTED BREATHING? ANXIOUSNESS? TENSION? GUT ISSUES? CHEST/BODY PAINS? WITHDRAWN?

ON THE OTHER HAND, WHAT DID GO WELL TODAY?

WHAT CONTRIBUTED TO THINGS GOING WELL?

READ WHAT YOU WROTE ABOVE...WHAT DO YOU THINK YOU NEED TO #DoBetter ON PURPOSE TOMORROW?

MIND DUMP, PROCESS & UNRAVEL

If you have Accountability **YOU HAVE OWNERSHIP!**

MY DAILY NEWSLETTER
SELF REFLECTION = SELF AWARENESS

WHAT'S 1 THING IN THE *OUTSIDE* WORLD THAT AFFECTED ME TODAY?

WHAT ARE 1-2 THINGS I AM CONTENT WITH IN MY LIFE TODAY? THANKFUL? GRATEFUL?

WHAT 3 THINGS WENT ON TODAY IN *MY WORLD* THAT STOOD OUT? WHAT MADE AN IMPACT?

WHAT DIDN'T GO WELL TODAY?

HOW DID I FEEL EMOTIONALLY? WRITE THEM OUT

HOW DID YOU FEEL PHYSICALLY? WHAT DO I NEED TO ADDRESS?
RESTRICTED BREATHING? ANXIOUSNESS? TENSION? GUT ISSUES? CHEST/BODY PAINS? WITHDRAWN?

ON THE OTHER HAND, WHAT DID GO WELL TODAY?

WHAT CONTRIBUTED TO THINGS GOING WELL?

READ WHAT YOU WROTE ABOVE...WHAT DO YOU THINK YOU NEED TO #DoBetter ON PURPOSE TOMORROW?

MIND DUMP, PROCESS & UNRAVEL

If you have Accountability **YOU HAVE OWNERSHIP!**

MY DAILY NEWSLETTER
SELF REFLECTION = SELF AWARENESS

WHAT'S 1 THING IN THE *OUTSIDE* WORLD THAT AFFECTED ME TODAY?

WHAT ARE 1-2 THINGS I AM CONTENT WITH IN MY LIFE TODAY? THANKFUL? GRATEFUL?

WHAT 3 THINGS WENT ON TODAY IN *MY WORLD* THAT STOOD OUT? WHAT MADE AN IMPACT?

_____   _____   _____

WHAT DIDN'T GO WELL TODAY?

HOW DID I FEEL EMOTIONALLY? WRITE THEM OUT

— ▬▬▬▬▬ +

HOW DID YOU FEEL PHYSICALLY? WHAT DO I NEED TO ADDRESS?
RESTRICTED BREATHING? ANXIOUSNESS? TENSION? GUT ISSUES? CHEST/BODY PAINS? WITHDRAWN?

ON THE OTHER HAND, WHAT DID GO WELL TODAY?

WHAT CONTRIBUTED TO THINGS GOING WELL?

READ WHAT YOU WROTE ABOVE…WHAT DO YOU THINK YOU NEED TO #DoBetter ON PURPOSE TOMORROW?

MIND DUMP, PROCESS & UNRAVEL

If you have Accountability **YOU HAVE OWNERSHIP!**

MY DAILY NEWSLETTER
SELF REFLECTION = SELF AWARENESS

WHAT'S 1 THING IN THE *OUTSIDE* WORLD THAT AFFECTED ME TODAY?

WHAT ARE 1-2 THINGS I AM CONTENT WITH IN MY LIFE TODAY? THANKFUL? GRATEFUL?

WHAT 3 THINGS WENT ON TODAY IN *MY WORLD* THAT STOOD OUT? WHAT MADE AN IMPACT?

WHAT DIDN'T GO WELL TODAY?

HOW DID I FEEL EMOTIONALLY? WRITE THEM OUT

HOW DID YOU FEEL PHYSICALLY? WHAT DO I NEED TO ADDRESS?
RESTRICTED BREATHING? ANXIOUSNESS? TENSION? GUT ISSUES? CHEST/BODY PAINS? WITHDRAWN?

ON THE OTHER HAND, WHAT DID GO WELL TODAY?

WHAT CONTRIBUTED TO THINGS GOING WELL?

READ WHAT YOU WROTE ABOVE...WHAT DO YOU THINK YOU NEED TO #DoBetter ON PURPOSE TOMORROW?

MIND DUMP, PROCESS & UNRAVEL

If you have Accountability **YOU HAVE OWNERSHIP!**

MY DAILY NEWSLETTER
SELF REFLECTION = SELF AWARENESS

WHAT'S 1 THING IN THE *OUTSIDE* WORLD THAT AFFECTED ME TODAY?

WHAT ARE 1-2 THINGS I AM CONTENT WITH IN MY LIFE TODAY? THANKFUL? GRATEFUL?

WHAT 3 THINGS WENT ON TODAY IN *MY WORLD* THAT STOOD OUT? WHAT MADE AN IMPACT?

WHAT DIDN'T GO WELL TODAY?

HOW DID I FEEL EMOTIONALLY? WRITE THEM OUT

HOW DID YOU FEEL PHYSICALLY? WHAT DO I NEED TO ADDRESS?
RESTRICTED BREATHING? ANXIOUSNESS? TENSION? GUT ISSUES? CHEST/BODY PAINS? WITHDRAWN?

ON THE OTHER HAND, WHAT DID GO WELL TODAY?

WHAT CONTRIBUTED TO THINGS GOING WELL?

READ WHAT YOU WROTE ABOVE...WHAT DO YOU THINK YOU NEED TO #DoBetter ON PURPOSE TOMORROW?

MIND DUMP, PROCESS & UNRAVEL

If you have Accountability **YOU HAVE OWNERSHIP!**

MY DAILY NEWSLETTER
SELF REFLECTION = SELF AWARENESS

WHAT'S 1 THING IN THE *OUTSIDE* WORLD THAT AFFECTED ME TODAY?

WHAT ARE 1-2 THINGS I AM CONTENT WITH IN MY LIFE TODAY? THANKFUL? GRATEFUL?

WHAT 3 THINGS WENT ON TODAY IN *MY WORLD* THAT STOOD OUT? WHAT MADE AN IMPACT?

WHAT DIDN'T GO WELL TODAY?

HOW DID I FEEL EMOTIONALLY? WRITE THEM OUT

HOW DID YOU FEEL PHYSICALLY? WHAT DO I NEED TO ADDRESS?
RESTRICTED BREATHING? ANXIOUSNESS? TENSION? GUT ISSUES? CHEST/BODY PAINS? WITHDRAWN?

ON THE OTHER HAND, WHAT DID GO WELL TODAY?

WHAT CONTRIBUTED TO THINGS GOING WELL?

READ WHAT YOU WROTE ABOVE...WHAT DO YOU THINK YOU NEED TO #DoBetter ON PURPOSE TOMORROW?

MIND DUMP, PROCESS & UNRAVEL

If you have Accountability **YOU HAVE OWNERSHIP!**

MY DAILY NEWSLETTER
SELF REFLECTION = SELF AWARENESS

WHAT'S 1 THING IN THE *OUTSIDE* WORLD THAT AFFECTED ME TODAY?

WHAT ARE 1-2 THINGS I AM CONTENT WITH IN MY LIFE TODAY? THANKFUL? GRATEFUL?

WHAT 3 THINGS WENT ON TODAY IN *MY WORLD* THAT STOOD OUT? WHAT MADE AN IMPACT?

_____   _____   _____

WHAT DIDN'T GO WELL TODAY?

HOW DID I FEEL EMOTIONALLY? WRITE THEM OUT

HOW DID YOU FEEL PHYSICALLY? WHAT DO I NEED TO ADDRESS?
RESTRICTED BREATHING? ANXIOUSNESS? TENSION? GUT ISSUES? CHEST/BODY PAINS? WITHDRAWN?

ON THE OTHER HAND, WHAT DID GO WELL TODAY?

WHAT CONTRIBUTED TO THINGS GOING WELL?

READ WHAT YOU WROTE ABOVE...WHAT DO YOU THINK YOU NEED TO #DoBetter ON PURPOSE TOMORROW?

MIND DUMP, PROCESS & UNRAVEL

If you have Accountability **YOU HAVE OWNERSHIP!**

MY DAILY NEWSLETTER
SELF REFLECTION = SELF AWARENESS

WHAT'S 1 THING IN THE *OUTSIDE* WORLD THAT AFFECTED ME TODAY?

WHAT ARE 1-2 THINGS I AM CONTENT WITH IN MY LIFE TODAY? THANKFUL? GRATEFUL?

WHAT 3 THINGS WENT ON TODAY IN *MY WORLD* THAT STOOD OUT? WHAT MADE AN IMPACT?

WHAT DIDN'T GO WELL TODAY?

HOW DID I FEEL EMOTIONALLY? WRITE THEM OUT

HOW DID YOU FEEL PHYSICALLY? WHAT DO I NEED TO ADDRESS?
RESTRICTED BREATHING? ANXIOUSNESS? TENSION? GUT ISSUES? CHEST/BODY PAINS? WITHDRAWN?

ON THE OTHER HAND, WHAT DID GO WELL TODAY?

WHAT CONTRIBUTED TO THINGS GOING WELL?

READ WHAT YOU WROTE ABOVE...WHAT DO YOU THINK YOU NEED TO #DoBetter ON PURPOSE TOMORROW?

MIND DUMP, PROCESS & UNRAVEL

If you have Accountability **YOU HAVE OWNERSHIP!**

MY DAILY NEWSLETTER
SELF REFLECTION = SELF AWARENESS

WHAT'S 1 THING IN THE *OUTSIDE* WORLD THAT AFFECTED ME TODAY?

WHAT ARE 1-2 THINGS I AM CONTENT WITH IN MY LIFE TODAY? THANKFUL? GRATEFUL?

WHAT 3 THINGS WENT ON TODAY IN *MY WORLD* THAT STOOD OUT? WHAT MADE AN IMPACT?

WHAT DIDN'T GO WELL TODAY?

HOW DID I FEEL EMOTIONALLY? WRITE THEM OUT

HOW DID YOU FEEL PHYSICALLY? WHAT DO I NEED TO ADDRESS?
RESTRICTED BREATHING? ANXIOUSNESS? TENSION? GUT ISSUES? CHEST/BODY PAINS? WITHDRAWN?

ON THE OTHER HAND, WHAT DID GO WELL TODAY?

WHAT CONTRIBUTED TO THINGS GOING WELL?

READ WHAT YOU WROTE ABOVE…WHAT DO YOU THINK YOU NEED TO #DoBetter ON PURPOSE TOMORROW?

MIND DUMP, PROCESS & UNRAVEL

If you have Accountability **YOU HAVE OWNERSHIP!**

MY DAILY NEWSLETTER
SELF REFLECTION = SELF AWARENESS

WHAT'S 1 THING IN THE *OUTSIDE* WORLD THAT AFFECTED ME TODAY?

WHAT ARE 1-2 THINGS I AM CONTENT WITH IN MY LIFE TODAY? THANKFUL? GRATEFUL?

WHAT 3 THINGS WENT ON TODAY IN *MY WORLD* THAT STOOD OUT? WHAT MADE AN IMPACT?

WHAT DIDN'T GO WELL TODAY?

HOW DID I FEEL EMOTIONALLY? WRITE THEM OUT

HOW DID YOU FEEL PHYSICALLY? WHAT DO I NEED TO ADDRESS?
RESTRICTED BREATHING? ANXIOUSNESS? TENSION? GUT ISSUES? CHEST/BODY PAINS? WITHDRAWN?

ON THE OTHER HAND, WHAT DID GO WELL TODAY?

WHAT CONTRIBUTED TO THINGS GOING WELL?

READ WHAT YOU WROTE ABOVE...WHAT DO YOU THINK YOU NEED TO #DoBetter ON PURPOSE TOMORROW?

MIND DUMP, PROCESS & UNRAVEL

If you have Accountability YOU HAVE OWNERSHIP!

MY DAILY NEWSLETTER
SELF REFLECTION = SELF AWARENESS

WHAT'S 1 THING IN THE *OUTSIDE* WORLD THAT AFFECTED ME TODAY?

WHAT ARE 1-2 THINGS I AM CONTENT WITH IN MY LIFE TODAY? THANKFUL? GRATEFUL?

WHAT 3 THINGS WENT ON TODAY IN *MY WORLD* THAT STOOD OUT? WHAT MADE AN IMPACT?

WHAT DIDN'T GO WELL TODAY?

HOW DID I FEEL EMOTIONALLY? WRITE THEM OUT

HOW DID YOU FEEL PHYSICALLY? WHAT DO I NEED TO ADDRESS?
RESTRICTED BREATHING? ANXIOUSNESS? TENSION? GUT ISSUES? CHEST/BODY PAINS? WITHDRAWN?

ON THE OTHER HAND, WHAT DID GO WELL TODAY?

WHAT CONTRIBUTED TO THINGS GOING WELL?

READ WHAT YOU WROTE ABOVE…WHAT DO YOU THINK YOU NEED TO #DoBetter ON PURPOSE TOMORROW?

MIND DUMP, PROCESS & UNRAVEL

If you take Responsibility
YOU HAVE OWNERSHIP!

ANSWER THESE QUESTIONS BELOW TO DEFINE YOUR PLAN FORWARD NEXT MONTH

WHERE DO YOU NEED TO DRAW A LINE TO #DOBETTER ON PURPOSE?

_____
_____
_____
_____
_____

WHAT HABIT DO YOU NEED TO WORK ON TO #DOBETTER ON PURPOSE?

_____
_____

WHAT'S 1 EMOTION I WILL I FOCUS ON TO GET UNDER CONTROL?

WHAT WILL MOTIVATE YOU TO #DOBETTER ON PURPOSE?

_____
_____
_____
_____
_____
_____

WHAT NEEDS TO BE UNRAVELED ABOUT THIS PAST MONTH?

_____
_____
_____
_____
_____
_____

MIND DUMP, PROCESS & UNRAVEL

Self Awareness Alignment

OUTLINE IN THESE CATEGORIES WHERE YOU WILL *FOCUS* YOUR SELF REFLECTION
WHAT THINGS WILL YOU KEEP IN THE FRONT OF YOUR MIND?

RELATIONSHIPS

HEALTH

FINANCES

LESIURE

CAREER

SPIRITUALITY

GROWTH

NOTES:

_____
_____

Intentional Habits
HOW WILL YOU BE INTENTIONAL?

REMEBER THESE IN YOUR DAILY REFLECTIONS

MORNING HABITS *MID-DAY HABITS* *EVENING HABITS*

WHAT **DISCIPLINES** WILL YOU PUT INTO PLACE?

WHAT WILL BE YOUR **WINNING STRATEGIE**S TO CHANGE WHAT YOU SEE ON A DAILY BASIS?

TRY: PRAYER/MEDITATION, WRITTEN REMINDERS, AND ACCOUNTABILITY PARTNERS…

WRITE BELOW 2-3 THINGS YOU ARE WILLING TO COMMIT TO DOING TO CHANGE BEHAVIORS (THINK IT, SPEAK IT, WRITE IT, WORK IT)

➤

➤

➤

If you have Accountability **YOU HAVE OWNERSHIP!**

MY DAILY NEWSLETTER
SELF REFLECTION = SELF AWARENESS

WHAT'S 1 THING IN THE *OUTSIDE* WORLD THAT AFFECTED ME TODAY?

WHAT ARE 1-2 THINGS I AM CONTENT WITH IN MY LIFE TODAY? THANKFUL? GRATEFUL?

WHAT 3 THINGS WENT ON TODAY IN *MY WORLD* THAT STOOD OUT? WHAT MADE AN IMPACT?

_____   _____   _____

WHAT DIDN'T GO WELL TODAY?

HOW DID I FEEL EMOTIONALLY? WRITE THEM OUT

HOW DID YOU FEEL PHYSICALLY? WHAT DO I NEED TO ADDRESS?
RESTRICTED BREATHING? ANXIOUSNESS? TENSION? GUT ISSUES? CHEST/BODY PAINS? WITHDRAWN?

ON THE OTHER HAND, WHAT DID GO WELL TODAY?

WHAT CONTRIBUTED TO THINGS GOING WELL?

READ WHAT YOU WROTE ABOVE...WHAT DO YOU THINK YOU NEED TO #DoBetter ON PURPOSE TOMORROW?

MIND DUMP, PROCESS & UNRAVEL

If you have Accountability **YOU HAVE OWNERSHIP!**

MY DAILY NEWSLETTER
SELF REFLECTION = SELF AWARENESS

WHAT'S 1 THING IN THE *OUTSIDE* WORLD THAT AFFECTED ME TODAY?

WHAT ARE 1-2 THINGS I AM CONTENT WITH IN MY LIFE TODAY? THANKFUL? GRATEFUL?

WHAT 3 THINGS WENT ON TODAY IN *MY WORLD* THAT STOOD OUT? WHAT MADE AN IMPACT?

_____   _____   _____

WHAT DIDN'T GO WELL TODAY?

HOW DID I FEEL EMOTIONALLY? WRITE THEM OUT

HOW DID YOU FEEL PHYSICALLY? WHAT DO I NEED TO ADDRESS?
RESTRICTED BREATHING? ANXIOUSNESS? TENSION? GUT ISSUES? CHEST/BODY PAINS? WITHDRAWN?

ON THE OTHER HAND, WHAT DID GO WELL TODAY?

WHAT CONTRIBUTED TO THINGS GOING WELL?

READ WHAT YOU WROTE ABOVE…WHAT DO YOU THINK YOU NEED TO #DoBetter ON PURPOSE TOMORROW?

MIND DUMP, PROCESS & UNRAVEL

If you have Accountability **YOU HAVE OWNERSHIP!**

MY DAILY NEWSLETTER
SELF REFLECTION = SELF AWARENESS

WHAT'S 1 THING IN THE *OUTSIDE* WORLD THAT AFFECTED ME TODAY?

WHAT ARE 1-2 THINGS I AM CONTENT WITH IN MY LIFE TODAY? THANKFUL? GRATEFUL?

WHAT 3 THINGS WENT ON TODAY IN *MY WORLD* THAT STOOD OUT? WHAT MADE AN IMPACT?

WHAT DIDN'T GO WELL TODAY?

HOW DID I FEEL EMOTIONALLY? WRITE THEM OUT

HOW DID YOU FEEL PHYSICALLY? WHAT DO I NEED TO ADDRESS?
RESTRICTED BREATHING? ANXIOUSNESS? TENSION? GUT ISSUES? CHEST/BODY PAINS? WITHDRAWN?

ON THE OTHER HAND, WHAT DID GO WELL TODAY?

WHAT CONTRIBUTED TO THINGS GOING WELL?

READ WHAT YOU WROTE ABOVE...WHAT DO YOU THINK YOU NEED TO #DoBetter ON PURPOSE TOMORROW?

MIND DUMP, PROCESS & UNRAVEL

If you have Accountability **YOU HAVE OWNERSHIP!**

MY DAILY NEWSLETTER
SELF REFLECTION = SELF AWARENESS

WHAT'S 1 THING IN THE *OUTSIDE* WORLD THAT AFFECTED ME TODAY?

WHAT ARE 1-2 THINGS I AM CONTENT WITH IN MY LIFE TODAY? THANKFUL? GRATEFUL?

WHAT 3 THINGS WENT ON TODAY IN *MY WORLD* THAT STOOD OUT? WHAT MADE AN IMPACT?

_____   _____   _____

WHAT DIDN'T GO WELL TODAY?

HOW DID I FEEL EMOTIONALLY? WRITE THEM OUT

HOW DID YOU FEEL PHYSICALLY? WHAT DO I NEED TO ADDRESS?
RESTRICTED BREATHING? ANXIOUSNESS? TENSION? GUT ISSUES? CHEST/BODY PAINS? WITHDRAWN?

ON THE OTHER HAND, WHAT DID GO WELL TODAY?

WHAT CONTRIBUTED TO THINGS GOING WELL?

READ WHAT YOU WROTE ABOVE…WHAT DO YOU THINK YOU NEED TO #DoBetter ON PURPOSE TOMORROW?

MIND DUMP, PROCESS & UNRAVEL

If you have Accountability **YOU HAVE OWNERSHIP!**

MY DAILY NEWSLETTER
SELF REFLECTION = SELF AWARENESS

WHAT'S 1 THING IN THE *OUTSIDE* WORLD THAT AFFECTED ME TODAY?

WHAT ARE 1-2 THINGS I AM CONTENT WITH IN MY LIFE TODAY? THANKFUL? GRATEFUL?

WHAT 3 THINGS WENT ON TODAY IN *MY WORLD* THAT STOOD OUT? WHAT MADE AN IMPACT?

WHAT DIDN'T GO WELL TODAY?

HOW DID I FEEL EMOTIONALLY? WRITE THEM OUT

HOW DID YOU FEEL PHYSICALLY? WHAT DO I NEED TO ADDRESS?
RESTRICTED BREATHING? ANXIOUSNESS? TENSION? GUT ISSUES? CHEST/BODY PAINS? WITHDRAWN?

ON THE OTHER HAND, WHAT DID GO WELL TODAY?

WHAT CONTRIBUTED TO THINGS GOING WELL?

READ WHAT YOU WROTE ABOVE...WHAT DO YOU THINK YOU NEED TO #DoBetter ON PURPOSE TOMORROW?

MIND DUMP, PROCESS & UNRAVEL

If you have Accountability **YOU HAVE OWNERSHIP!**

MY DAILY NEWSLETTER
SELF REFLECTION = SELF AWARENESS

WHAT'S 1 THING IN THE *OUTSIDE* WORLD THAT AFFECTED ME TODAY?

WHAT ARE 1-2 THINGS I AM CONTENT WITH IN MY LIFE TODAY? THANKFUL? GRATEFUL?

WHAT 3 THINGS WENT ON TODAY IN *MY WORLD* THAT STOOD OUT? WHAT MADE AN IMPACT?

WHAT DIDN'T GO WELL TODAY?

HOW DID I FEEL EMOTIONALLY? WRITE THEM OUT

HOW DID YOU FEEL PHYSICALLY? WHAT DO I NEED TO ADDRESS?
RESTRICTED BREATHING? ANXIOUSNESS? TENSION? GUT ISSUES? CHEST/BODY PAINS? WITHDRAWN?

ON THE OTHER HAND, WHAT DID GO WELL TODAY?

WHAT CONTRIBUTED TO THINGS GOING WELL?

READ WHAT YOU WROTE ABOVE…WHAT DO YOU THINK YOU NEED TO #DoBetter ON PURPOSE TOMORROW?

MIND DUMP, PROCESS & UNRAVEL

If you have Accountability **YOU HAVE OWNERSHIP!**

MY DAILY NEWSLETTER
SELF REFLECTION = SELF AWARENESS

WHAT'S 1 THING IN THE *OUTSIDE* WORLD THAT AFFECTED ME TODAY?

WHAT ARE 1-2 THINGS I AM CONTENT WITH IN MY LIFE TODAY? THANKFUL? GRATEFUL?

WHAT 3 THINGS WENT ON TODAY IN *MY WORLD* THAT STOOD OUT? WHAT MADE AN IMPACT?

WHAT DIDN'T GO WELL TODAY?

HOW DID I FEEL EMOTIONALLY? WRITE THEM OUT

HOW DID YOU FEEL PHYSICALLY? WHAT DO I NEED TO ADDRESS?
RESTRICTED BREATHING? ANXIOUSNESS? TENSION? GUT ISSUES? CHEST/BODY PAINS? WITHDRAWN?

ON THE OTHER HAND, WHAT DID GO WELL TODAY?

WHAT CONTRIBUTED TO THINGS GOING WELL?

READ WHAT YOU WROTE ABOVE...WHAT DO YOU THINK YOU NEED TO #DoBETTER ON PURPOSE TOMORROW?

MIND DUMP, PROCESS & UNRAVEL

If you have Accountability **YOU HAVE OWNERSHIP!**

MY DAILY NEWSLETTER
SELF REFLECTION = SELF AWARENESS

What's 1 thing in the *OUTSIDE* world that Affected me today?

What are 1-2 things I am content with in my life today? Thankful? Grateful?

What 3 things went on today in *My world* that stood out? What made an impact?

What didn't go well today?

How did I feel emotionally? Write them out

How did you feel physically? What do I need to address? Restricted Breathing? Anxiousness? Tension? Gut issues? Chest/Body Pains? Withdrawn?

On the other hand, What did go well today?

What contributed to things going well?

Read what you wrote above…What do you think you need to #DoBetter on Purpose Tomorrow?

MIND DUMP, PROCESS & UNRAVEL

If you have Accountability **YOU HAVE OWNERSHIP!**

MY DAILY NEWSLETTER
SELF REFLECTION = SELF AWARENESS

WHAT'S 1 THING IN THE *OUTSIDE* WORLD THAT AFFECTED ME TODAY?

WHAT ARE 1-2 THINGS I AM CONTENT WITH IN MY LIFE TODAY? THANKFUL? GRATEFUL?

WHAT 3 THINGS WENT ON TODAY IN *MY WORLD* THAT STOOD OUT? WHAT MADE AN IMPACT?

WHAT DIDN'T GO WELL TODAY?

HOW DID I FEEL EMOTIONALLY? WRITE THEM OUT

HOW DID YOU FEEL PHYSICALLY? WHAT DO I NEED TO ADDRESS?
RESTRICTED BREATHING? ANXIOUSNESS? TENSION? GUT ISSUES? CHEST/BODY PAINS? WITHDRAWN?

ON THE OTHER HAND, WHAT DID GO WELL TODAY?

WHAT CONTRIBUTED TO THINGS GOING WELL?

READ WHAT YOU WROTE ABOVE...WHAT DO YOU THINK YOU NEED TO #DoBETTER ON PURPOSE TOMORROW?

MIND DUMP, PROCESS & UNRAVEL

If you have Accountability **YOU HAVE OWNERSHIP!**

MY DAILY NEWSLETTER
SELF REFLECTION = SELF AWARENESS

WHAT'S 1 THING IN THE *OUTSIDE* WORLD THAT AFFECTED ME TODAY?

WHAT ARE 1-2 THINGS I AM CONTENT WITH IN MY LIFE TODAY? THANKFUL? GRATEFUL?

WHAT 3 THINGS WENT ON TODAY IN *MY WORLD* THAT STOOD OUT? WHAT MADE AN IMPACT?

_____   _____   _____

WHAT DIDN'T GO WELL TODAY?

HOW DID I FEEL EMOTIONALLY? WRITE THEM OUT

HOW DID YOU FEEL PHYSICALLY? WHAT DO I NEED TO ADDRESS?
RESTRICTED BREATHING? ANXIOUSNESS? TENSION? GUT ISSUES? CHEST/BODY PAINS? WITHDRAWN?

ON THE OTHER HAND, WHAT DID GO WELL TODAY?

WHAT CONTRIBUTED TO THINGS GOING WELL?

READ WHAT YOU WROTE ABOVE...WHAT DO YOU THINK YOU NEED TO #DoBetter ON PURPOSE TOMORROW?

MIND DUMP, PROCESS & UNRAVEL

If you have Accountability **YOU HAVE OWNERSHIP!**

MY DAILY NEWSLETTER
SELF REFLECTION = SELF AWARENESS

WHAT'S 1 THING IN THE *OUTSIDE* WORLD THAT AFFECTED ME TODAY?

WHAT ARE 1-2 THINGS I AM CONTENT WITH IN MY LIFE TODAY? THANKFUL? GRATEFUL?

WHAT 3 THINGS WENT ON TODAY IN *MY WORLD* THAT STOOD OUT? WHAT MADE AN IMPACT?

WHAT DIDN'T GO WELL TODAY?

HOW DID I FEEL EMOTIONALLY? WRITE THEM OUT

HOW DID YOU FEEL PHYSICALLY? WHAT DO I NEED TO ADDRESS?
RESTRICTED BREATHING? ANXIOUSNESS? TENSION? GUT ISSUES? CHEST/BODY PAINS? WITHDRAWN?

ON THE OTHER HAND, WHAT DID GO WELL TODAY?

WHAT CONTRIBUTED TO THINGS GOING WELL?

READ WHAT YOU WROTE ABOVE...WHAT DO YOU THINK YOU NEED TO #DoBetter ON PURPOSE TOMORROW?

MIND DUMP, PROCESS & UNRAVEL

If you have Accountability **YOU HAVE OWNERSHIP!**

MY DAILY NEWSLETTER
SELF REFLECTION = SELF AWARENESS

WHAT'S 1 THING IN THE *OUTSIDE* WORLD THAT AFFECTED ME TODAY?

WHAT ARE 1-2 THINGS I AM CONTENT WITH IN MY LIFE TODAY? THANKFUL? GRATEFUL?

WHAT 3 THINGS WENT ON TODAY IN *MY WORLD* THAT STOOD OUT? WHAT MADE AN IMPACT?

WHAT DIDN'T GO WELL TODAY?

HOW DID I FEEL EMOTIONALLY? WRITE THEM OUT

HOW DID YOU FEEL PHYSICALLY? WHAT DO I NEED TO ADDRESS?
RESTRICTED BREATHING? ANXIOUSNESS? TENSION? GUT ISSUES? CHEST/BODY PAINS? WITHDRAWN?

ON THE OTHER HAND, WHAT DID GO WELL TODAY?

WHAT CONTRIBUTED TO THINGS GOING WELL?

READ WHAT YOU WROTE ABOVE…WHAT DO YOU THINK YOU NEED TO #DoBetter ON PURPOSE TOMORROW?

MIND DUMP, PROCESS & UNRAVEL

If you have Accountability **YOU HAVE OWNERSHIP!**

MY DAILY NEWSLETTER
SELF REFLECTION = SELF AWARENESS

WHAT'S 1 THING IN THE *OUTSIDE* WORLD THAT AFFECTED ME TODAY?

WHAT ARE 1-2 THINGS I AM CONTENT WITH IN MY LIFE TODAY? THANKFUL? GRATEFUL?

WHAT 3 THINGS WENT ON TODAY IN *MY WORLD* THAT STOOD OUT? WHAT MADE AN IMPACT?

WHAT DIDN'T GO WELL TODAY?

HOW DID I FEEL EMOTIONALLY? WRITE THEM OUT

HOW DID YOU FEEL PHYSICALLY? WHAT DO I NEED TO ADDRESS?
RESTRICTED BREATHING? ANXIOUSNESS? TENSION? GUT ISSUES? CHEST/BODY PAINS? WITHDRAWN?

ON THE OTHER HAND, WHAT DID GO WELL TODAY?

WHAT CONTRIBUTED TO THINGS GOING WELL?

READ WHAT YOU WROTE ABOVE...WHAT DO YOU THINK YOU NEED TO #DoBetter ON PURPOSE TOMORROW?

MIND DUMP, PROCESS & UNRAVEL

If you have Accountability **YOU HAVE OWNERSHIP!**

MY DAILY NEWSLETTER
SELF REFLECTION = SELF AWARENESS

WHAT'S 1 THING IN THE *OUTSIDE* WORLD THAT AFFECTED ME TODAY?

WHAT ARE 1-2 THINGS I AM CONTENT WITH IN MY LIFE TODAY? THANKFUL? GRATEFUL?

WHAT 3 THINGS WENT ON TODAY IN *MY WORLD* THAT STOOD OUT? WHAT MADE AN IMPACT?

WHAT DIDN'T GO WELL TODAY?

HOW DID I FEEL EMOTIONALLY? WRITE THEM OUT

HOW DID YOU FEEL PHYSICALLY? WHAT DO I NEED TO ADDRESS?
RESTRICTED BREATHING? ANXIOUSNESS? TENSION? GUT ISSUES? CHEST/BODY PAINS? WITHDRAWN?

ON THE OTHER HAND, WHAT DID GO WELL TODAY?

WHAT CONTRIBUTED TO THINGS GOING WELL?

READ WHAT YOU WROTE ABOVE...WHAT DO YOU THINK YOU NEED TO #DoBetter ON PURPOSE TOMORROW?

MIND DUMP, PROCESS & UNRAVEL

If you have Accountability **YOU HAVE OWNERSHIP!**

MY DAILY NEWSLETTER
SELF REFLECTION = SELF AWARENESS

WHAT'S 1 THING IN THE *OUTSIDE* WORLD THAT AFFECTED ME TODAY?

WHAT ARE 1-2 THINGS I AM CONTENT WITH IN MY LIFE TODAY? THANKFUL? GRATEFUL?

WHAT 3 THINGS WENT ON TODAY IN *MY WORLD* THAT STOOD OUT? WHAT MADE AN IMPACT?

WHAT DIDN'T GO WELL TODAY?

HOW DID I FEEL EMOTIONALLY? WRITE THEM OUT

HOW DID YOU FEEL PHYSICALLY? WHAT DO I NEED TO ADDRESS?
RESTRICTED BREATHING? ANXIOUSNESS? TENSION? GUT ISSUES? CHEST/BODY PAINS? WITHDRAWN?

ON THE OTHER HAND, WHAT DID GO WELL TODAY?

WHAT CONTRIBUTED TO THINGS GOING WELL?

READ WHAT YOU WROTE ABOVE...WHAT DO YOU THINK YOU NEED TO #DoBetter ON PURPOSE TOMORROW?

MIND DUMP, PROCESS & UNRAVEL

If you have Accountability **YOU HAVE OWNERSHIP!**

MY DAILY NEWSLETTER
SELF REFLECTION = SELF AWARENESS

WHAT'S 1 THING IN THE *OUTSIDE* WORLD THAT AFFECTED ME TODAY?

WHAT ARE 1-2 THINGS I AM CONTENT WITH IN MY LIFE TODAY? THANKFUL? GRATEFUL?

WHAT 3 THINGS WENT ON TODAY IN *MY WORLD* THAT STOOD OUT? WHAT MADE AN IMPACT?

WHAT DIDN'T GO WELL TODAY?

HOW DID I FEEL EMOTIONALLY? WRITE THEM OUT

HOW DID YOU FEEL PHYSICALLY? WHAT DO I NEED TO ADDRESS?
RESTRICTED BREATHING? ANXIOUSNESS? TENSION? GUT ISSUES? CHEST/BODY PAINS? WITHDRAWN?

ON THE OTHER HAND, WHAT DID GO WELL TODAY?

WHAT CONTRIBUTED TO THINGS GOING WELL?

READ WHAT YOU WROTE ABOVE…WHAT DO YOU THINK YOU NEED TO #DoBetter ON PURPOSE TOMORROW?

MIND DUMP, PROCESS & UNRAVEL

If you have Accountability **YOU HAVE OWNERSHIP!**

MY DAILY NEWSLETTER
SELF REFLECTION = SELF AWARENESS

WHAT'S 1 THING IN THE *OUTSIDE* WORLD THAT AFFECTED ME TODAY?

WHAT ARE 1-2 THINGS I AM CONTENT WITH IN MY LIFE TODAY? THANKFUL? GRATEFUL?

WHAT 3 THINGS WENT ON TODAY IN *MY WORLD* THAT STOOD OUT? WHAT MADE AN IMPACT?

WHAT DIDN'T GO WELL TODAY?

HOW DID I FEEL EMOTIONALLY? WRITE THEM OUT

HOW DID YOU FEEL PHYSICALLY? WHAT DO I NEED TO ADDRESS?
RESTRICTED BREATHING? ANXIOUSNESS? TENSION? GUT ISSUES? CHEST/BODY PAINS? WITHDRAWN?

ON THE OTHER HAND, WHAT DID GO WELL TODAY?

WHAT CONTRIBUTED TO THINGS GOING WELL?

READ WHAT YOU WROTE ABOVE...WHAT DO YOU THINK YOU NEED TO #DoBetter ON PURPOSE TOMORROW?

MIND DUMP, PROCESS & UNRAVEL

If you have Accountability **YOU HAVE OWNERSHIP!**

MY DAILY NEWSLETTER
SELF REFLECTION = SELF AWARENESS

WHAT'S 1 THING IN THE *OUTSIDE* WORLD THAT AFFECTED ME TODAY?

WHAT ARE 1-2 THINGS I AM CONTENT WITH IN MY LIFE TODAY? THANKFUL? GRATEFUL?

WHAT 3 THINGS WENT ON TODAY IN *MY WORLD* THAT STOOD OUT? WHAT MADE AN IMPACT?

WHAT DIDN'T GO WELL TODAY?

HOW DID I FEEL EMOTIONALLY? WRITE THEM OUT

HOW DID YOU FEEL PHYSICALLY? WHAT DO I NEED TO ADDRESS?
RESTRICTED BREATHING? ANXIOUSNESS? TENSION? GUT ISSUES? CHEST/BODY PAINS? WITHDRAWN?

ON THE OTHER HAND, WHAT DID GO WELL TODAY?

WHAT CONTRIBUTED TO THINGS GOING WELL?

READ WHAT YOU WROTE ABOVE...WHAT DO YOU THINK YOU NEED TO #DoBetter ON PURPOSE TOMORROW?

MIND DUMP, PROCESS & UNRAVEL

If you have Accountability **YOU HAVE OWNERSHIP!**

MY DAILY NEWSLETTER
SELF REFLECTION = SELF AWARENESS

WHAT'S 1 THING IN THE *OUTSIDE* WORLD THAT AFFECTED ME TODAY?

WHAT ARE 1-2 THINGS I AM CONTENT WITH IN MY LIFE TODAY? THANKFUL? GRATEFUL?

WHAT 3 THINGS WENT ON TODAY IN *MY WORLD* THAT STOOD OUT? WHAT MADE AN IMPACT?

WHAT DIDN'T GO WELL TODAY?

HOW DID I FEEL EMOTIONALLY? WRITE THEM OUT

HOW DID YOU FEEL PHYSICALLY? WHAT DO I NEED TO ADDRESS?
RESTRICTED BREATHING? ANXIOUSNESS? TENSION? GUT ISSUES? CHEST/BODY PAINS? WITHDRAWN?

ON THE OTHER HAND, WHAT DID GO WELL TODAY?

WHAT CONTRIBUTED TO THINGS GOING WELL?

READ WHAT YOU WROTE ABOVE... WHAT DO YOU THINK YOU NEED TO #DoBetter ON PURPOSE TOMORROW?

MIND DUMP, PROCESS & UNRAVEL

If you have Accountability **YOU HAVE OWNERSHIP!**

MY DAILY NEWSLETTER
SELF REFLECTION = SELF AWARENESS

WHAT'S 1 THING IN THE *OUTSIDE* WORLD THAT AFFECTED ME TODAY?

WHAT ARE 1-2 THINGS I AM CONTENT WITH IN MY LIFE TODAY? THANKFUL? GRATEFUL?

WHAT 3 THINGS WENT ON TODAY IN *MY WORLD* THAT STOOD OUT? WHAT MADE AN IMPACT?

WHAT DIDN'T GO WELL TODAY?

HOW DID I FEEL EMOTIONALLY? WRITE THEM OUT

HOW DID YOU FEEL PHYSICALLY? WHAT DO I NEED TO ADDRESS?
RESTRICTED BREATHING? ANXIOUSNESS? TENSION? GUT ISSUES? CHEST/BODY PAINS? WITHDRAWN?

ON THE OTHER HAND, WHAT DID GO WELL TODAY?

WHAT CONTRIBUTED TO THINGS GOING WELL?

READ WHAT YOU WROTE ABOVE...WHAT DO YOU THINK YOU NEED TO #DoBetter ON PURPOSE TOMORROW?

MIND DUMP, PROCESS & UNRAVEL

If you have Accountability **YOU HAVE OWNERSHIP!**

MY DAILY NEWSLETTER
SELF REFLECTION = SELF AWARENESS

WHAT'S 1 THING IN THE *OUTSIDE* WORLD THAT AFFECTED ME TODAY?

WHAT ARE 1-2 THINGS I AM CONTENT WITH IN MY LIFE TODAY? THANKFUL? GRATEFUL?

WHAT 3 THINGS WENT ON TODAY IN *MY WORLD* THAT STOOD OUT? WHAT MADE AN IMPACT?

WHAT DIDN'T GO WELL TODAY?

HOW DID I FEEL EMOTIONALLY? WRITE THEM OUT

HOW DID YOU FEEL PHYSICALLY? WHAT DO I NEED TO ADDRESS?
RESTRICTED BREATHING? ANXIOUSNESS? TENSION? GUT ISSUES? CHEST/BODY PAINS? WITHDRAWN?

ON THE OTHER HAND, WHAT DID GO WELL TODAY?

WHAT CONTRIBUTED TO THINGS GOING WELL?

READ WHAT YOU WROTE ABOVE...WHAT DO YOU THINK YOU NEED TO #DoBetter ON PURPOSE TOMORROW?

MIND DUMP, PROCESS & UNRAVEL

If you have Accountability **YOU HAVE OWNERSHIP!**

MY DAILY NEWSLETTER
SELF REFLECTION = SELF AWARENESS

WHAT'S 1 THING IN THE *OUTSIDE* WORLD THAT AFFECTED ME TODAY?

WHAT ARE 1-2 THINGS I AM CONTENT WITH IN MY LIFE TODAY? THANKFUL? GRATEFUL?

WHAT 3 THINGS WENT ON TODAY IN *MY WORLD* THAT STOOD OUT? WHAT MADE AN IMPACT?

WHAT DIDN'T GO WELL TODAY?

HOW DID I FEEL EMOTIONALLY? WRITE THEM OUT

HOW DID YOU FEEL PHYSICALLY? WHAT DO I NEED TO ADDRESS? RESTRICTED BREATHING? ANXIOUSNESS? TENSION? GUT ISSUES? CHEST/BODY PAINS? WITHDRAWN?

ON THE OTHER HAND, WHAT DID GO WELL TODAY?

WHAT CONTRIBUTED TO THINGS GOING WELL?

READ WHAT YOU WROTE ABOVE…WHAT DO YOU THINK YOU NEED TO #DoBetter ON PURPOSE TOMORROW?

MIND DUMP, PROCESS & UNRAVEL

If you have Accountability **YOU HAVE OWNERSHIP!**

MY DAILY NEWSLETTER
SELF REFLECTION = SELF AWARENESS

WHAT'S 1 THING IN THE *OUTSIDE* WORLD THAT AFFECTED ME TODAY?

WHAT ARE 1-2 THINGS I AM CONTENT WITH IN MY LIFE TODAY? THANKFUL? GRATEFUL?

WHAT 3 THINGS WENT ON TODAY IN *MY WORLD* THAT STOOD OUT? WHAT MADE AN IMPACT?

WHAT DIDN'T GO WELL TODAY?

HOW DID I FEEL EMOTIONALLY? WRITE THEM OUT

HOW DID YOU FEEL PHYSICALLY? WHAT DO I NEED TO ADDRESS?
RESTRICTED BREATHING? ANXIOUSNESS? TENSION? GUT ISSUES? CHEST/BODY PAINS? WITHDRAWN?

ON THE OTHER HAND, WHAT DID GO WELL TODAY?

WHAT CONTRIBUTED TO THINGS GOING WELL?

READ WHAT YOU WROTE ABOVE... WHAT DO YOU THINK YOU NEED TO #DoBetter ON PURPOSE TOMORROW?

MIND DUMP, PROCESS & UNRAVEL

If you have Accountability **YOU HAVE OWNERSHIP!**

MY DAILY NEWSLETTER
SELF REFLECTION = SELF AWARENESS

WHAT'S 1 THING IN THE *OUTSIDE* WORLD THAT AFFECTED ME TODAY?

WHAT ARE 1-2 THINGS I AM CONTENT WITH IN MY LIFE TODAY? THANKFUL? GRATEFUL?

WHAT 3 THINGS WENT ON TODAY IN *MY WORLD* THAT STOOD OUT? WHAT MADE AN IMPACT?

_____ _____ _____

WHAT DIDN'T GO WELL TODAY?

HOW DID I FEEL EMOTIONALLY? WRITE THEM OUT

HOW DID YOU FEEL PHYSICALLY? WHAT DO I NEED TO ADDRESS?
RESTRICTED BREATHING? ANXIOUSNESS? TENSION? GUT ISSUES? CHEST/BODY PAINS? WITHDRAWN?

ON THE OTHER HAND, WHAT DID GO WELL TODAY?

WHAT CONTRIBUTED TO THINGS GOING WELL?

READ WHAT YOU WROTE ABOVE...WHAT DO YOU THINK YOU NEED TO #DoBetter ON PURPOSE TOMORROW?

MIND DUMP, PROCESS & UNRAVEL

If you have Accountability **YOU HAVE OWNERSHIP!**

MY DAILY NEWSLETTER
SELF REFLECTION = SELF AWARENESS

WHAT'S 1 THING IN THE *OUTSIDE* WORLD THAT AFFECTED ME TODAY?

WHAT ARE 1-2 THINGS I AM CONTENT WITH IN MY LIFE TODAY? THANKFUL? GRATEFUL?

WHAT 3 THINGS WENT ON TODAY IN *MY WORLD* THAT STOOD OUT? WHAT MADE AN IMPACT?

WHAT DIDN'T GO WELL TODAY?

HOW DID I FEEL EMOTIONALLY? WRITE THEM OUT

HOW DID YOU FEEL PHYSICALLY? WHAT DO I NEED TO ADDRESS?
RESTRICTED BREATHING? ANXIOUSNESS? TENSION? GUT ISSUES? CHEST/BODY PAINS? WITHDRAWN?

ON THE OTHER HAND, WHAT DID GO WELL TODAY?

WHAT CONTRIBUTED TO THINGS GOING WELL?

READ WHAT YOU WROTE ABOVE…WHAT DO YOU THINK YOU NEED TO #DoBetter ON PURPOSE TOMORROW?

MIND DUMP, PROCESS & UNRAVEL

If you have Accountability **YOU HAVE OWNERSHIP!**

MY DAILY NEWSLETTER
SELF REFLECTION = SELF AWARENESS

WHAT'S 1 THING IN THE *OUTSIDE* WORLD THAT AFFECTED ME TODAY?

WHAT ARE 1-2 THINGS I AM CONTENT WITH IN MY LIFE TODAY? THANKFUL? GRATEFUL?

WHAT 3 THINGS WENT ON TODAY IN *MY WORLD* THAT STOOD OUT? WHAT MADE AN IMPACT?

_____   _____   _____

WHAT DIDN'T GO WELL TODAY?

HOW DID I FEEL EMOTIONALLY? WRITE THEM OUT

− ▬▬▬▬▬▬▬▬▬▬ +

HOW DID YOU FEEL PHYSICALLY? WHAT DO I NEED TO ADDRESS?
RESTRICTED BREATHING? ANXIOUSNESS? TENSION? GUT ISSUES? CHEST/BODY PAINS? WITHDRAWN?

ON THE OTHER HAND, WHAT DID GO WELL TODAY?

WHAT CONTRIBUTED TO THINGS GOING WELL?

READ WHAT YOU WROTE ABOVE…WHAT DO YOU THINK YOU NEED TO #DOBETTER ON PURPOSE TOMORROW?

MIND DUMP, PROCESS & UNRAVEL

If you have Accountability **YOU HAVE OWNERSHIP!**

MY DAILY NEWSLETTER
SELF REFLECTION = SELF AWARENESS

WHAT'S 1 THING IN THE *OUTSIDE* WORLD THAT AFFECTED ME TODAY?

WHAT ARE 1-2 THINGS I AM CONTENT WITH IN MY LIFE TODAY? THANKFUL? GRATEFUL?

WHAT 3 THINGS WENT ON TODAY IN *MY WORLD* THAT STOOD OUT? WHAT MADE AN IMPACT?

WHAT DIDN'T GO WELL TODAY?

HOW DID I FEEL EMOTIONALLY? WRITE THEM OUT

HOW DID YOU FEEL PHYSICALLY? WHAT DO I NEED TO ADDRESS?
RESTRICTED BREATHING? ANXIOUSNESS? TENSION? GUT ISSUES? CHEST/BODY PAINS? WITHDRAWN?

ON THE OTHER HAND, WHAT DID GO WELL TODAY?

WHAT CONTRIBUTED TO THINGS GOING WELL?

READ WHAT YOU WROTE ABOVE… WHAT DO YOU THINK YOU NEED TO #DoBetter ON PURPOSE TOMORROW?

MIND DUMP, PROCESS & UNRAVEL

If you have Accountability **YOU HAVE OWNERSHIP!**

MY DAILY NEWSLETTER
SELF REFLECTION = SELF AWARENESS

WHAT'S 1 THING IN THE *OUTSIDE* WORLD THAT AFFECTED ME TODAY?

WHAT ARE 1-2 THINGS I AM CONTENT WITH IN MY LIFE TODAY? THANKFUL? GRATEFUL?

WHAT 3 THINGS WENT ON TODAY IN *MY WORLD* THAT STOOD OUT? WHAT MADE AN IMPACT?

_____   _____   _____

WHAT DIDN'T GO WELL TODAY?

HOW DID I FEEL EMOTIONALLY? WRITE THEM OUT

HOW DID YOU FEEL PHYSICALLY? WHAT DO I NEED TO ADDRESS?
RESTRICTED BREATHING? ANXIOUSNESS? TENSION? GUT ISSUES? CHEST/BODY PAINS? WITHDRAWN?

ON THE OTHER HAND, WHAT DID GO WELL TODAY?

WHAT CONTRIBUTED TO THINGS GOING WELL?

READ WHAT YOU WROTE ABOVE…WHAT DO YOU THINK YOU NEED TO #DoBetter ON PURPOSE TOMORROW?

MIND DUMP, PROCESS & UNRAVEL

If you have Accountability **YOU HAVE OWNERSHIP!**

MY DAILY NEWSLETTER
SELF REFLECTION = SELF AWARENESS

WHAT'S 1 THING IN THE *OUTSIDE* WORLD THAT AFFECTED ME TODAY?

WHAT ARE 1-2 THINGS I AM CONTENT WITH IN MY LIFE TODAY? THANKFUL? GRATEFUL?

WHAT 3 THINGS WENT ON TODAY IN *MY WORLD* THAT STOOD OUT? WHAT MADE AN IMPACT?

WHAT DIDN'T GO WELL TODAY?

HOW DID I FEEL EMOTIONALLY? WRITE THEM OUT

HOW DID YOU FEEL PHYSICALLY? WHAT DO I NEED TO ADDRESS?
RESTRICTED BREATHING? ANXIOUSNESS? TENSION? GUT ISSUES? CHEST/BODY PAINS? WITHDRAWN?

ON THE OTHER HAND, WHAT DID GO WELL TODAY?

WHAT CONTRIBUTED TO THINGS GOING WELL?

READ WHAT YOU WROTE ABOVE...WHAT DO YOU THINK YOU NEED TO #DOBETTER ON PURPOSE TOMORROW?

MIND DUMP, PROCESS & UNRAVEL

If you have Accountability **YOU HAVE OWNERSHIP!**

MY DAILY NEWSLETTER
SELF REFLECTION = SELF AWARENESS

WHAT'S 1 THING IN THE *OUTSIDE* WORLD THAT AFFECTED ME TODAY?

WHAT ARE 1-2 THINGS I AM CONTENT WITH IN MY LIFE TODAY? THANKFUL? GRATEFUL?

WHAT 3 THINGS WENT ON TODAY IN *MY WORLD* THAT STOOD OUT? WHAT MADE AN IMPACT?

WHAT DIDN'T GO WELL TODAY?

HOW DID I FEEL EMOTIONALLY? WRITE THEM OUT

HOW DID YOU FEEL PHYSICALLY? WHAT DO I NEED TO ADDRESS?
RESTRICTED BREATHING? ANXIOUSNESS? TENSION? GUT ISSUES? CHEST/BODY PAINS? WITHDRAWN?

ON THE OTHER HAND, WHAT DID GO WELL TODAY?

WHAT CONTRIBUTED TO THINGS GOING WELL?

READ WHAT YOU WROTE ABOVE...WHAT DO YOU THINK YOU NEED TO #DoBetter ON PURPOSE TOMORROW?

MIND DUMP, PROCESS & UNRAVEL

If you have Accountability **YOU HAVE OWNERSHIP!**

MY DAILY NEWSLETTER
SELF REFLECTION = SELF AWARENESS

WHAT'S 1 THING IN THE *OUTSIDE* WORLD THAT AFFECTED ME TODAY?

WHAT ARE 1-2 THINGS I AM CONTENT WITH IN MY LIFE TODAY? THANKFUL? GRATEFUL?

WHAT 3 THINGS WENT ON TODAY IN *MY WORLD* THAT STOOD OUT? WHAT MADE AN IMPACT?

_____   _____   _____

WHAT DIDN'T GO WELL TODAY?

HOW DID I FEEL EMOTIONALLY? WRITE THEM OUT

− ———————————— +

HOW DID YOU FEEL PHYSICALLY? WHAT DO I NEED TO ADDRESS?
RESTRICTED BREATHING? ANXIOUSNESS? TENSION? GUT ISSUES? CHEST/BODY PAINS? WITHDRAWN?

ON THE OTHER HAND, WHAT DID GO WELL TODAY?

WHAT CONTRIBUTED TO THINGS GOING WELL?

READ WHAT YOU WROTE ABOVE... WHAT DO YOU THINK YOU NEED TO #DoBetter ON PURPOSE TOMORROW?

MIND DUMP, PROCESS & UNRAVEL

If you take Responsibility
YOU HAVE OWNERSHIP!
ANSWER THESE QUESTIONS BELOW TO DEFINE YOUR PLAN FORWARD NEXT MONTH

WHERE DO YOU NEED TO DRAW A LINE TO #DOBETTER ON PURPOSE?

_____

_____

_____

_____

_____

WHAT HABIT DO YOU NEED TO WORK ON TO #DOBETTER ON PURPOSE?

_____

_____

WHAT'S 1 EMOTION I WILL I FOCUS ON TO GET UNDER CONTROL?

WHAT WILL MOTIVATE YOU TO #DOBETTER ON PURPOSE?

_____

_____

_____

_____

_____

_____

WHAT NEEDS TO BE UNRAVELED ABOUT THIS PAST MONTH?

_____

_____

_____

_____

_____

_____

MIND DUMP, PROCESS & UNRAVEL

Self Awareness Alignment

OUTLINE IN THESE CATEGORIES WHERE YOU WILL *FOCUS* YOUR SELF REFLECTION
WHAT THINGS WILL YOU KEEP IN THE FRONT OF YOUR MIND?

RELATIONSHIPS	HEALTH

FINANCES	LESIURE	CAREER

SPIRITUALITY	GROWTH

NOTES:
_____
_____

Intentional Habits
HOW WILL YOU BE INTENTIONAL?

REMEBER THESE IN YOUR DAILY REFLECTIONS

MORNING HABITS	MID-DAY HABITS	EVENING HABITS

What **DISCIPLINES** will you put into place?

What will be your **WINNING STRATEGIE**S to change what you see on a daily basis?

Try: Prayer/meditation, written reminders, and accountability partners...

Write below 2-3 things you are willing to commit to doing to change behaviors (Think it, Speak it, Write it, Work it)

➤

➤

➤

If you have Accountability **YOU HAVE OWNERSHIP!**

MY DAILY NEWSLETTER
SELF REFLECTION = SELF AWARENESS

WHAT'S 1 THING IN THE *OUTSIDE* WORLD THAT AFFECTED ME TODAY?

WHAT ARE 1-2 THINGS I AM CONTENT WITH IN MY LIFE TODAY? THANKFUL? GRATEFUL?

WHAT 3 THINGS WENT ON TODAY IN *MY WORLD* THAT STOOD OUT? WHAT MADE AN IMPACT?

WHAT DIDN'T GO WELL TODAY?

HOW DID I FEEL EMOTIONALLY? WRITE THEM OUT

HOW DID YOU FEEL PHYSICALLY? WHAT DO I NEED TO ADDRESS?
RESTRICTED BREATHING? ANXIOUSNESS? TENSION? GUT ISSUES? CHEST/BODY PAINS? WITHDRAWN?

ON THE OTHER HAND, WHAT DID GO WELL TODAY?

WHAT CONTRIBUTED TO THINGS GOING WELL?

READ WHAT YOU WROTE ABOVE...WHAT DO YOU THINK YOU NEED TO #DOBETTER ON PURPOSE TOMORROW?

MIND DUMP, PROCESS & UNRAVEL

If you have Accountability **YOU HAVE OWNERSHIP!**

MY DAILY NEWSLETTER
SELF REFLECTION = SELF AWARENESS

WHAT'S 1 THING IN THE *OUTSIDE* WORLD THAT AFFECTED ME TODAY?

WHAT ARE 1-2 THINGS I AM CONTENT WITH IN MY LIFE TODAY? THANKFUL? GRATEFUL?

WHAT 3 THINGS WENT ON TODAY IN *MY WORLD* THAT STOOD OUT? WHAT MADE AN IMPACT?

WHAT DIDN'T GO WELL TODAY?

HOW DID I FEEL EMOTIONALLY? WRITE THEM OUT

HOW DID YOU FEEL PHYSICALLY? WHAT DO I NEED TO ADDRESS?
RESTRICTED BREATHING? ANXIOUSNESS? TENSION? GUT ISSUES? CHEST/BODY PAINS? WITHDRAWN?

ON THE OTHER HAND, WHAT DID GO WELL TODAY?

WHAT CONTRIBUTED TO THINGS GOING WELL?

READ WHAT YOU WROTE ABOVE…WHAT DO YOU THINK YOU NEED TO #DoBetter ON PURPOSE TOMORROW?

MIND DUMP, PROCESS & UNRAVEL

If you have Accountability **YOU HAVE OWNERSHIP!**

MY DAILY NEWSLETTER
SELF REFLECTION = SELF AWARENESS

WHAT'S 1 THING IN THE *OUTSIDE* WORLD THAT AFFECTED ME TODAY?

WHAT ARE 1-2 THINGS I AM CONTENT WITH IN MY LIFE TODAY? THANKFUL? GRATEFUL?

WHAT 3 THINGS WENT ON TODAY IN *MY WORLD* THAT STOOD OUT? WHAT MADE AN IMPACT?

WHAT DIDN'T GO WELL TODAY?

HOW DID I FEEL EMOTIONALLY? WRITE THEM OUT

HOW DID YOU FEEL PHYSICALLY? WHAT DO I NEED TO ADDRESS?
RESTRICTED BREATHING? ANXIOUSNESS? TENSION? GUT ISSUES? CHEST/BODY PAINS? WITHDRAWN?

ON THE OTHER HAND, WHAT DID GO WELL TODAY?

WHAT CONTRIBUTED TO THINGS GOING WELL?

READ WHAT YOU WROTE ABOVE...WHAT DO YOU THINK YOU NEED TO #DOBETTER ON PURPOSE TOMORROW?

MIND DUMP, PROCESS & UNRAVEL

If you have Accountability **YOU HAVE OWNERSHIP!**

MY DAILY NEWSLETTER
SELF REFLECTION = SELF AWARENESS

WHAT'S 1 THING IN THE *OUTSIDE* WORLD THAT AFFECTED ME TODAY?

WHAT ARE 1-2 THINGS I AM CONTENT WITH IN MY LIFE TODAY? THANKFUL? GRATEFUL?

WHAT 3 THINGS WENT ON TODAY IN *MY WORLD* THAT STOOD OUT? WHAT MADE AN IMPACT?

_____   _____   _____

WHAT DIDN'T GO WELL TODAY?

HOW DID I FEEL EMOTIONALLY? WRITE THEM OUT

– ———————————— +

HOW DID YOU FEEL PHYSICALLY? WHAT DO I NEED TO ADDRESS?
RESTRICTED BREATHING? ANXIOUSNESS? TENSION? GUT ISSUES? CHEST/BODY PAINS? WITHDRAWN?

ON THE OTHER HAND, WHAT DID GO WELL TODAY?

WHAT CONTRIBUTED TO THINGS GOING WELL?

READ WHAT YOU WROTE ABOVE... WHAT DO YOU THINK YOU NEED TO #DoBetter ON PURPOSE TOMORROW?

MIND DUMP, PROCESS & UNRAVEL

If you have Accountability **YOU HAVE OWNERSHIP!**

MY DAILY NEWSLETTER
SELF REFLECTION = SELF AWARENESS

WHAT'S 1 THING IN THE *OUTSIDE* WORLD THAT AFFECTED ME TODAY?

WHAT ARE 1-2 THINGS I AM CONTENT WITH IN MY LIFE TODAY? THANKFUL? GRATEFUL?

WHAT 3 THINGS WENT ON TODAY IN *MY WORLD* THAT STOOD OUT? WHAT MADE AN IMPACT?

WHAT DIDN'T GO WELL TODAY?

HOW DID I FEEL EMOTIONALLY? WRITE THEM OUT

HOW DID YOU FEEL PHYSICALLY? WHAT DO I NEED TO ADDRESS?
RESTRICTED BREATHING? ANXIOUSNESS? TENSION? GUT ISSUES? CHEST/BODY PAINS? WITHDRAWN?

ON THE OTHER HAND, WHAT DID GO WELL TODAY?

WHAT CONTRIBUTED TO THINGS GOING WELL?

READ WHAT YOU WROTE ABOVE…WHAT DO YOU THINK YOU NEED TO #DoBetter ON PURPOSE TOMORROW?

MIND DUMP, PROCESS & UNRAVEL

If you have Accountability **YOU HAVE OWNERSHIP!**

MY DAILY NEWSLETTER
SELF REFLECTION = SELF AWARENESS

WHAT'S 1 THING IN THE *OUTSIDE* WORLD THAT AFFECTED ME TODAY?

WHAT ARE 1-2 THINGS I AM CONTENT WITH IN MY LIFE TODAY? THANKFUL? GRATEFUL?

WHAT 3 THINGS WENT ON TODAY IN *MY WORLD* THAT STOOD OUT? WHAT MADE AN IMPACT?

WHAT DIDN'T GO WELL TODAY?

HOW DID I FEEL EMOTIONALLY? WRITE THEM OUT

HOW DID YOU FEEL PHYSICALLY? WHAT DO I NEED TO ADDRESS?
RESTRICTED BREATHING? ANXIOUSNESS? TENSION? GUT ISSUES? CHEST/BODY PAINS? WITHDRAWN?

ON THE OTHER HAND, WHAT DID GO WELL TODAY?

WHAT CONTRIBUTED TO THINGS GOING WELL?

READ WHAT YOU WROTE ABOVE...WHAT DO YOU THINK YOU NEED TO #DoBetter ON PURPOSE TOMORROW?

MIND DUMP, PROCESS & UNRAVEL

If you have Accountability **YOU HAVE OWNERSHIP!**

MY DAILY NEWSLETTER
SELF REFLECTION = SELF AWARENESS

WHAT'S 1 THING IN THE *OUTSIDE* WORLD THAT AFFECTED ME TODAY?

WHAT ARE 1-2 THINGS I AM CONTENT WITH IN MY LIFE TODAY? THANKFUL? GRATEFUL?

WHAT 3 THINGS WENT ON TODAY IN *MY WORLD* THAT STOOD OUT? WHAT MADE AN IMPACT?

WHAT DIDN'T GO WELL TODAY?

HOW DID I FEEL EMOTIONALLY? WRITE THEM OUT

HOW DID YOU FEEL PHYSICALLY? WHAT DO I NEED TO ADDRESS?
RESTRICTED BREATHING? ANXIOUSNESS? TENSION? GUT ISSUES? CHEST/BODY PAINS? WITHDRAWN?

ON THE OTHER HAND, WHAT DID GO WELL TODAY?

WHAT CONTRIBUTED TO THINGS GOING WELL?

READ WHAT YOU WROTE ABOVE...WHAT DO YOU THINK YOU NEED TO #DoBetter ON PURPOSE TOMORROW?

MIND DUMP, PROCESS & UNRAVEL

If you have Accountability **YOU HAVE OWNERSHIP!**

MY DAILY NEWSLETTER
SELF REFLECTION = SELF AWARENESS

WHAT'S 1 THING IN THE *OUTSIDE* WORLD THAT AFFECTED ME TODAY?

WHAT ARE 1-2 THINGS I AM CONTENT WITH IN MY LIFE TODAY? THANKFUL? GRATEFUL?

WHAT 3 THINGS WENT ON TODAY IN *MY WORLD* THAT STOOD OUT? WHAT MADE AN IMPACT?

_____   _____   _____

WHAT DIDN'T GO WELL TODAY?

HOW DID I FEEL EMOTIONALLY? WRITE THEM OUT

HOW DID YOU FEEL PHYSICALLY? WHAT DO I NEED TO ADDRESS?
RESTRICTED BREATHING? ANXIOUSNESS? TENSION? GUT ISSUES? CHEST/BODY PAINS? WITHDRAWN?

ON THE OTHER HAND, WHAT DID GO WELL TODAY?

WHAT CONTRIBUTED TO THINGS GOING WELL?

READ WHAT YOU WROTE ABOVE...WHAT DO YOU THINK YOU NEED TO #DoBetter ON PURPOSE TOMORROW?

MIND DUMP, PROCESS & UNRAVEL

If you have Accountability **YOU HAVE OWNERSHIP!**

MY DAILY NEWSLETTER
SELF REFLECTION = SELF AWARENESS

WHAT'S 1 THING IN THE *OUTSIDE* WORLD THAT AFFECTED ME TODAY?
_____

WHAT ARE 1-2 THINGS I AM CONTENT WITH IN MY LIFE TODAY? THANKFUL? GRATEFUL?

WHAT 3 THINGS WENT ON TODAY IN *MY WORLD* THAT STOOD OUT? WHAT MADE AN IMPACT?

_____ _____ _____

WHAT DIDN'T GO WELL TODAY?
_____
_____
_____
_____

HOW DID I FEEL EMOTIONALLY? WRITE THEM OUT
😠 😟 😐 🙂 😊
− ▬▬▬▬▬▬▬▬▬▬ +
_____
_____
_____
_____

HOW DID YOU FEEL PHYSICALLY? WHAT DO I NEED TO ADDRESS?
RESTRICTED BREATHING? ANXIOUSNESS? TENSION? GUT ISSUES? CHEST/BODY PAINS? WITHDRAWN?
_____

ON THE OTHER HAND, WHAT DID GO WELL TODAY?
_____
_____
_____
_____
_____

WHAT CONTRIBUTED TO THINGS GOING WELL?
_____
_____
_____
_____
_____

READ WHAT YOU WROTE ABOVE...WHAT DO YOU THINK YOU NEED TO #DoBetter ON PURPOSE TOMORROW?
_____
_____

MIND DUMP, PROCESS & UNRAVEL

If you have Accountability **YOU HAVE OWNERSHIP!**

MY DAILY NEWSLETTER
SELF REFLECTION = SELF AWARENESS

WHAT'S 1 THING IN THE *OUTSIDE* WORLD THAT AFFECTED ME TODAY?

WHAT ARE 1-2 THINGS I AM CONTENT WITH IN MY LIFE TODAY? THANKFUL? GRATEFUL?

WHAT 3 THINGS WENT ON TODAY IN *MY WORLD* THAT STOOD OUT? WHAT MADE AN IMPACT?

WHAT DIDN'T GO WELL TODAY?

HOW DID I FEEL EMOTIONALLY? WRITE THEM OUT

HOW DID YOU FEEL PHYSICALLY? WHAT DO I NEED TO ADDRESS?
RESTRICTED BREATHING? ANXIOUSNESS? TENSION? GUT ISSUES? CHEST/BODY PAINS? WITHDRAWN?

ON THE OTHER HAND, WHAT DID GO WELL TODAY?

WHAT CONTRIBUTED TO THINGS GOING WELL?

READ WHAT YOU WROTE ABOVE...WHAT DO YOU THINK YOU NEED TO #DoBetter ON PURPOSE TOMORROW?

MIND DUMP, PROCESS & UNRAVEL

If you have Accountability **YOU HAVE OWNERSHIP!**

MY DAILY NEWSLETTER
SELF REFLECTION = SELF AWARENESS

WHAT'S 1 THING IN THE *OUTSIDE* WORLD THAT AFFECTED ME TODAY?

WHAT ARE 1-2 THINGS I AM CONTENT WITH IN MY LIFE TODAY? THANKFUL? GRATEFUL?

WHAT 3 THINGS WENT ON TODAY IN *MY WORLD* THAT STOOD OUT? WHAT MADE AN IMPACT?

WHAT DIDN'T GO WELL TODAY?

HOW DID I FEEL EMOTIONALLY? WRITE THEM OUT

— +

HOW DID YOU FEEL PHYSICALLY? WHAT DO I NEED TO ADDRESS?
RESTRICTED BREATHING? ANXIOUSNESS? TENSION? GUT ISSUES? CHEST/BODY PAINS? WITHDRAWN?

ON THE OTHER HAND, WHAT DID GO WELL TODAY?

WHAT CONTRIBUTED TO THINGS GOING WELL?

READ WHAT YOU WROTE ABOVE...WHAT DO YOU THINK YOU NEED TO #DoBetter ON PURPOSE TOMORROW?

MIND DUMP, PROCESS & UNRAVEL

If you have Accountability **YOU HAVE OWNERSHIP!**

MY DAILY NEWSLETTER
SELF REFLECTION = SELF AWARENESS

WHAT'S 1 THING IN THE *OUTSIDE* WORLD THAT AFFECTED ME TODAY?

WHAT ARE 1-2 THINGS I AM CONTENT WITH IN MY LIFE TODAY? THANKFUL? GRATEFUL?

WHAT 3 THINGS WENT ON TODAY IN *MY WORLD* THAT STOOD OUT? WHAT MADE AN IMPACT?

WHAT DIDN'T GO WELL TODAY?

HOW DID I FEEL EMOTIONALLY? WRITE THEM OUT

– ———— +

HOW DID YOU FEEL PHYSICALLY? WHAT DO I NEED TO ADDRESS?
RESTRICTED BREATHING? ANXIOUSNESS? TENSION? GUT ISSUES? CHEST/BODY PAINS? WITHDRAWN?

ON THE OTHER HAND, WHAT DID GO WELL TODAY?

WHAT CONTRIBUTED TO THINGS GOING WELL?

READ WHAT YOU WROTE ABOVE…WHAT DO YOU THINK YOU NEED TO #DoBetter ON PURPOSE TOMORROW?

MIND DUMP, PROCESS & UNRAVEL

If you have Accountability **YOU HAVE OWNERSHIP!**

MY DAILY NEWSLETTER
SELF REFLECTION = SELF AWARENESS

WHAT'S 1 THING IN THE *OUTSIDE* WORLD THAT AFFECTED ME TODAY?

WHAT ARE 1-2 THINGS I AM CONTENT WITH IN MY LIFE TODAY? THANKFUL? GRATEFUL?

WHAT 3 THINGS WENT ON TODAY IN *MY WORLD* THAT STOOD OUT? WHAT MADE AN IMPACT?

_____   _____   _____

WHAT DIDN'T GO WELL TODAY?

_____
_____
_____
_____

HOW DID I FEEL EMOTIONALLY? WRITE THEM OUT

— _____ +

_____
_____
_____

HOW DID YOU FEEL PHYSICALLY? WHAT DO I NEED TO ADDRESS?
RESTRICTED BREATHING? ANXIOUSNESS? TENSION? GUT ISSUES? CHEST/BODY PAINS? WITHDRAWN?

_____

ON THE OTHER HAND, WHAT DID GO WELL TODAY?

_____
_____
_____
_____
_____

WHAT CONTRIBUTED TO THINGS GOING WELL?

_____
_____
_____
_____
_____

READ WHAT YOU WROTE ABOVE…WHAT DO YOU THINK YOU NEED TO #DoBetter ON PURPOSE TOMORROW?

_____
_____

MIND DUMP, PROCESS & UNRAVEL

If you have Accountability **YOU HAVE OWNERSHIP!**

MY DAILY NEWSLETTER
SELF REFLECTION = SELF AWARENESS

WHAT'S 1 THING IN THE *OUTSIDE* WORLD THAT AFFECTED ME TODAY?

WHAT ARE 1-2 THINGS I AM CONTENT WITH IN MY LIFE TODAY? THANKFUL? GRATEFUL?

WHAT 3 THINGS WENT ON TODAY IN *MY WORLD* THAT STOOD OUT? WHAT MADE AN IMPACT?

WHAT DIDN'T GO WELL TODAY?

HOW DID I FEEL EMOTIONALLY? WRITE THEM OUT

HOW DID YOU FEEL PHYSICALLY? WHAT DO I NEED TO ADDRESS?
RESTRICTED BREATHING? ANXIOUSNESS? TENSION? GUT ISSUES? CHEST/BODY PAINS? WITHDRAWN?

ON THE OTHER HAND, WHAT DID GO WELL TODAY?

WHAT CONTRIBUTED TO THINGS GOING WELL?

READ WHAT YOU WROTE ABOVE...WHAT DO YOU THINK YOU NEED TO #DoBetter ON PURPOSE TOMORROW?

MIND DUMP, PROCESS & UNRAVEL

If you have Accountability **YOU HAVE OWNERSHIP!**

MY DAILY NEWSLETTER
SELF REFLECTION = SELF AWARENESS

WHAT'S 1 THING IN THE *OUTSIDE* WORLD THAT AFFECTED ME TODAY?

WHAT ARE 1-2 THINGS I AM CONTENT WITH IN MY LIFE TODAY? THANKFUL? GRATEFUL?

WHAT 3 THINGS WENT ON TODAY IN *MY WORLD* THAT STOOD OUT? WHAT MADE AN IMPACT?

_____   _____   _____

WHAT DIDN'T GO WELL TODAY?

HOW DID I FEEL EMOTIONALLY? WRITE THEM OUT

— +

HOW DID YOU FEEL PHYSICALLY? WHAT DO I NEED TO ADDRESS?
RESTRICTED BREATHING? ANXIOUSNESS? TENSION? GUT ISSUES? CHEST/BODY PAINS? WITHDRAWN?

ON THE OTHER HAND, WHAT DID GO WELL TODAY?

WHAT CONTRIBUTED TO THINGS GOING WELL?

READ WHAT YOU WROTE ABOVE...WHAT DO YOU THINK YOU NEED TO #DoBetter ON PURPOSE TOMORROW?

MIND DUMP, PROCESS & UNRAVEL

If you have Accountability **YOU HAVE OWNERSHIP!**

MY DAILY NEWSLETTER
SELF REFLECTION = SELF AWARENESS

WHAT'S 1 THING IN THE *OUTSIDE* WORLD THAT AFFECTED ME TODAY?

WHAT ARE 1-2 THINGS I AM CONTENT WITH IN MY LIFE TODAY? THANKFUL? GRATEFUL?

WHAT 3 THINGS WENT ON TODAY IN *MY WORLD* THAT STOOD OUT? WHAT MADE AN IMPACT?

WHAT DIDN'T GO WELL TODAY?

HOW DID I FEEL EMOTIONALLY? WRITE THEM OUT

HOW DID YOU FEEL PHYSICALLY? WHAT DO I NEED TO ADDRESS?
RESTRICTED BREATHING? ANXIOUSNESS? TENSION? GUT ISSUES? CHEST/BODY PAINS? WITHDRAWN?

ON THE OTHER HAND, WHAT DID GO WELL TODAY?

WHAT CONTRIBUTED TO THINGS GOING WELL?

READ WHAT YOU WROTE ABOVE...WHAT DO YOU THINK YOU NEED TO #DoBetter ON PURPOSE TOMORROW?

MIND DUMP, PROCESS & UNRAVEL

If you have Accountability **YOU HAVE OWNERSHIP!**

MY DAILY NEWSLETTER
SELF REFLECTION = SELF AWARENESS

WHAT'S 1 THING IN THE *OUTSIDE* WORLD THAT AFFECTED ME TODAY?

WHAT ARE 1-2 THINGS I AM CONTENT WITH IN MY LIFE TODAY? THANKFUL? GRATEFUL?

WHAT 3 THINGS WENT ON TODAY IN *MY WORLD* THAT STOOD OUT? WHAT MADE AN IMPACT?

WHAT DIDN'T GO WELL TODAY?

HOW DID I FEEL EMOTIONALLY? WRITE THEM OUT

HOW DID YOU FEEL PHYSICALLY? WHAT DO I NEED TO ADDRESS? RESTRICTED BREATHING? ANXIOUSNESS? TENSION? GUT ISSUES? CHEST/BODY PAINS? WITHDRAWN?

ON THE OTHER HAND, WHAT DID GO WELL TODAY?

WHAT CONTRIBUTED TO THINGS GOING WELL?

READ WHAT YOU WROTE ABOVE...WHAT DO YOU THINK YOU NEED TO #DoBetter ON PURPOSE TOMORROW?

MIND DUMP, PROCESS & UNRAVEL

If you have Accountability **YOU HAVE OWNERSHIP!**

MY DAILY NEWSLETTER
SELF REFLECTION = SELF AWARENESS

WHAT'S 1 THING IN THE *OUTSIDE* WORLD THAT AFFECTED ME TODAY?

WHAT ARE 1-2 THINGS I AM CONTENT WITH IN MY LIFE TODAY? THANKFUL? GRATEFUL?

WHAT 3 THINGS WENT ON TODAY IN *MY WORLD* THAT STOOD OUT? WHAT MADE AN IMPACT?

WHAT DIDN'T GO WELL TODAY?

HOW DID I FEEL EMOTIONALLY? WRITE THEM OUT

HOW DID YOU FEEL PHYSICALLY? WHAT DO I NEED TO ADDRESS?
RESTRICTED BREATHING? ANXIOUSNESS? TENSION? GUT ISSUES? CHEST/BODY PAINS? WITHDRAWN?

ON THE OTHER HAND, WHAT DID GO WELL TODAY?

WHAT CONTRIBUTED TO THINGS GOING WELL?

READ WHAT YOU WROTE ABOVE... WHAT DO YOU THINK YOU NEED TO #DoBetter ON PURPOSE TOMORROW?

MIND DUMP, PROCESS & UNRAVEL

If you have Accountability **YOU HAVE OWNERSHIP!**

MY DAILY NEWSLETTER
SELF REFLECTION = SELF AWARENESS

WHAT'S 1 THING IN THE *OUTSIDE* WORLD THAT AFFECTED ME TODAY?

WHAT ARE 1-2 THINGS I AM CONTENT WITH IN MY LIFE TODAY? THANKFUL? GRATEFUL?

WHAT 3 THINGS WENT ON TODAY IN *MY WORLD* THAT STOOD OUT? WHAT MADE AN IMPACT?

WHAT DIDN'T GO WELL TODAY?

HOW DID I FEEL EMOTIONALLY? WRITE THEM OUT

HOW DID YOU FEEL PHYSICALLY? WHAT DO I NEED TO ADDRESS?
RESTRICTED BREATHING? ANXIOUSNESS? TENSION? GUT ISSUES? CHEST/BODY PAINS? WITHDRAWN?

ON THE OTHER HAND, WHAT DID GO WELL TODAY?

WHAT CONTRIBUTED TO THINGS GOING WELL?

READ WHAT YOU WROTE ABOVE…WHAT DO YOU THINK YOU NEED TO #DoBetter ON PURPOSE TOMORROW?

MIND DUMP, PROCESS & UNRAVEL

If you have Accountability **YOU HAVE OWNERSHIP!**

MY DAILY NEWSLETTER
SELF REFLECTION = SELF AWARENESS

WHAT'S 1 THING IN THE *OUTSIDE* WORLD THAT AFFECTED ME TODAY?

WHAT ARE 1-2 THINGS I AM CONTENT WITH IN MY LIFE TODAY? THANKFUL? GRATEFUL?

WHAT 3 THINGS WENT ON TODAY IN *MY WORLD* THAT STOOD OUT? WHAT MADE AN IMPACT?

WHAT DIDN'T GO WELL TODAY?

HOW DID I FEEL EMOTIONALLY? WRITE THEM OUT

— +

HOW DID YOU FEEL PHYSICALLY? WHAT DO I NEED TO ADDRESS?
RESTRICTED BREATHING? ANXIOUSNESS? TENSION? GUT ISSUES? CHEST/BODY PAINS? WITHDRAWN?

ON THE OTHER HAND, WHAT DID GO WELL TODAY?

WHAT CONTRIBUTED TO THINGS GOING WELL?

READ WHAT YOU WROTE ABOVE…WHAT DO YOU THINK YOU NEED TO #DoBetter ON PURPOSE TOMORROW?

MIND DUMP, PROCESS & UNRAVEL

If you have Accountability **YOU HAVE OWNERSHIP!**

MY DAILY NEWSLETTER
SELF REFLECTION = SELF AWARENESS

WHAT'S 1 THING IN THE *OUTSIDE* WORLD THAT AFFECTED ME TODAY?

WHAT ARE 1-2 THINGS I AM CONTENT WITH IN MY LIFE TODAY? THANKFUL? GRATEFUL?

WHAT 3 THINGS WENT ON TODAY IN *MY WORLD* THAT STOOD OUT? WHAT MADE AN IMPACT?

_____   _____   _____

WHAT DIDN'T GO WELL TODAY?

HOW DID I FEEL EMOTIONALLY? WRITE THEM OUT

HOW DID YOU FEEL PHYSICALLY? WHAT DO I NEED TO ADDRESS?
RESTRICTED BREATHING? ANXIOUSNESS? TENSION? GUT ISSUES? CHEST/BODY PAINS? WITHDRAWN?

ON THE OTHER HAND, WHAT DID GO WELL TODAY?

WHAT CONTRIBUTED TO THINGS GOING WELL?

READ WHAT YOU WROTE ABOVE...WHAT DO YOU THINK YOU NEED TO #DoBetter ON PURPOSE TOMORROW?

MIND DUMP, PROCESS & UNRAVEL

If you have Accountability **YOU HAVE OWNERSHIP!**

MY DAILY NEWSLETTER
SELF REFLECTION = SELF AWARENESS

WHAT'S 1 THING IN THE *OUTSIDE* WORLD THAT AFFECTED ME TODAY?

WHAT ARE 1-2 THINGS I AM CONTENT WITH IN MY LIFE TODAY? THANKFUL? GRATEFUL?

WHAT 3 THINGS WENT ON TODAY IN *MY WORLD* THAT STOOD OUT? WHAT MADE AN IMPACT?

WHAT DIDN'T GO WELL TODAY?

HOW DID I FEEL EMOTIONALLY? WRITE THEM OUT

HOW DID YOU FEEL PHYSICALLY? WHAT DO I NEED TO ADDRESS?
RESTRICTED BREATHING? ANXIOUSNESS? TENSION? GUT ISSUES? CHEST/BODY PAINS? WITHDRAWN?

ON THE OTHER HAND, WHAT DID GO WELL TODAY?

WHAT CONTRIBUTED TO THINGS GOING WELL?

READ WHAT YOU WROTE ABOVE…WHAT DO YOU THINK YOU NEED TO #DoBetter ON PURPOSE TOMORROW?

MIND DUMP, PROCESS & UNRAVEL

If you have Accountability **YOU HAVE OWNERSHIP!**

MY DAILY NEWSLETTER
SELF REFLECTION = SELF AWARENESS

WHAT'S 1 THING IN THE *OUTSIDE* WORLD THAT AFFECTED ME TODAY?

WHAT ARE 1-2 THINGS I AM CONTENT WITH IN MY LIFE TODAY? THANKFUL? GRATEFUL?

WHAT 3 THINGS WENT ON TODAY IN *MY WORLD* THAT STOOD OUT? WHAT MADE AN IMPACT?

WHAT DIDN'T GO WELL TODAY?

HOW DID I FEEL EMOTIONALLY? WRITE THEM OUT

HOW DID YOU FEEL PHYSICALLY? WHAT DO I NEED TO ADDRESS?
RESTRICTED BREATHING? ANXIOUSNESS? TENSION? GUT ISSUES? CHEST/BODY PAINS? WITHDRAWN?

ON THE OTHER HAND, WHAT DID GO WELL TODAY?

WHAT CONTRIBUTED TO THINGS GOING WELL?

READ WHAT YOU WROTE ABOVE...WHAT DO YOU THINK YOU NEED TO #DoBetter ON PURPOSE TOMORROW?

MIND DUMP, PROCESS & UNRAVEL

If you have Accountability **YOU HAVE OWNERSHIP!**

MY DAILY NEWSLETTER
SELF REFLECTION = SELF AWARENESS

WHAT'S 1 THING IN THE *OUTSIDE* WORLD THAT AFFECTED ME TODAY?

WHAT ARE 1-2 THINGS I AM CONTENT WITH IN MY LIFE TODAY? THANKFUL? GRATEFUL?

WHAT 3 THINGS WENT ON TODAY IN *MY WORLD* THAT STOOD OUT? WHAT MADE AN IMPACT?

_____   _____   _____

WHAT DIDN'T GO WELL TODAY?

HOW DID I FEEL EMOTIONALLY? WRITE THEM OUT

— ————— +

HOW DID YOU FEEL PHYSICALLY? WHAT DO I NEED TO ADDRESS?
RESTRICTED BREATHING? ANXIOUSNESS? TENSION? GUT ISSUES? CHEST/BODY PAINS? WITHDRAWN?

ON THE OTHER HAND, WHAT DID GO WELL TODAY?

WHAT CONTRIBUTED TO THINGS GOING WELL?

READ WHAT YOU WROTE ABOVE… WHAT DO YOU THINK YOU NEED TO #DoBetter ON PURPOSE TOMORROW?

MIND DUMP, PROCESS & UNRAVEL

If you have Accountability **YOU HAVE OWNERSHIP!**

MY DAILY NEWSLETTER
SELF REFLECTION = SELF AWARENESS

WHAT'S 1 THING IN THE *OUTSIDE* WORLD THAT AFFECTED ME TODAY?
___

WHAT ARE 1-2 THINGS I AM CONTENT WITH IN MY LIFE TODAY? THANKFUL? GRATEFUL?

WHAT 3 THINGS WENT ON TODAY IN *MY WORLD* THAT STOOD OUT? WHAT MADE AN IMPACT?
_____   _____   _____

WHAT DIDN'T GO WELL TODAY?
___
___
___
___

HOW DID I FEEL EMOTIONALLY? WRITE THEM OUT
☹ 🙁 😐 🙂 😊
−   +
___
___
___

HOW DID YOU FEEL PHYSICALLY? WHAT DO I NEED TO ADDRESS?
RESTRICTED BREATHING? ANXIOUSNESS? TENSION? GUT ISSUES? CHEST/BODY PAINS? WITHDRAWN?
___

ON THE OTHER HAND, WHAT DID GO WELL TODAY?
___
___
___
___
___

WHAT CONTRIBUTED TO THINGS GOING WELL?
___
___
___
___
___

READ WHAT YOU WROTE ABOVE...WHAT DO YOU THINK YOU NEED TO #DOBETTER ON PURPOSE TOMORROW?
___
___

MIND DUMP, PROCESS & UNRAVEL

If you have Accountability **YOU HAVE OWNERSHIP!**

MY DAILY NEWSLETTER
SELF REFLECTION = SELF AWARENESS

WHAT'S 1 THING IN THE *OUTSIDE* WORLD THAT AFFECTED ME TODAY?

WHAT ARE 1-2 THINGS I AM CONTENT WITH IN MY LIFE TODAY? THANKFUL? GRATEFUL?

WHAT 3 THINGS WENT ON TODAY IN *MY WORLD* THAT STOOD OUT? WHAT MADE AN IMPACT?

WHAT DIDN'T GO WELL TODAY?

HOW DID I FEEL EMOTIONALLY? WRITE THEM OUT

HOW DID YOU FEEL PHYSICALLY? WHAT DO I NEED TO ADDRESS?
RESTRICTED BREATHING? ANXIOUSNESS? TENSION? GUT ISSUES? CHEST/BODY PAINS? WITHDRAWN?

ON THE OTHER HAND, WHAT DID GO WELL TODAY?

WHAT CONTRIBUTED TO THINGS GOING WELL?

READ WHAT YOU WROTE ABOVE... WHAT DO YOU THINK YOU NEED TO #DoBETTER ON PURPOSE TOMORROW?

MIND DUMP, PROCESS & UNRAVEL

If you have Accountability **YOU HAVE OWNERSHIP!**

MY DAILY NEWSLETTER
SELF REFLECTION = SELF AWARENESS

WHAT'S 1 THING IN THE *OUTSIDE* WORLD THAT AFFECTED ME TODAY?

WHAT ARE 1-2 THINGS I AM CONTENT WITH IN MY LIFE TODAY? THANKFUL? GRATEFUL?

WHAT 3 THINGS WENT ON TODAY IN *MY WORLD* THAT STOOD OUT? WHAT MADE AN IMPACT?

WHAT DIDN'T GO WELL TODAY?

HOW DID I FEEL EMOTIONALLY? WRITE THEM OUT

HOW DID YOU FEEL PHYSICALLY? WHAT DO I NEED TO ADDRESS? RESTRICTED BREATHING? ANXIOUSNESS? TENSION? GUT ISSUES? CHEST/BODY PAINS? WITHDRAWN?

ON THE OTHER HAND, WHAT DID GO WELL TODAY?

WHAT CONTRIBUTED TO THINGS GOING WELL?

READ WHAT YOU WROTE ABOVE…WHAT DO YOU THINK YOU NEED TO #DoBetter ON PURPOSE TOMORROW?

MIND DUMP, PROCESS & UNRAVEL

If you have Accountability **YOU HAVE OWNERSHIP!**

MY DAILY NEWSLETTER
SELF REFLECTION = SELF AWARENESS

WHAT'S 1 THING IN THE *OUTSIDE* WORLD THAT AFFECTED ME TODAY?

WHAT ARE 1-2 THINGS I AM CONTENT WITH IN MY LIFE TODAY? THANKFUL? GRATEFUL?

WHAT 3 THINGS WENT ON TODAY IN *MY WORLD* THAT STOOD OUT? WHAT MADE AN IMPACT?

_____   _____   _____

WHAT DIDN'T GO WELL TODAY?

HOW DID I FEEL EMOTIONALLY? WRITE THEM OUT

−　　　　　　　　　　＋

HOW DID YOU FEEL PHYSICALLY? WHAT DO I NEED TO ADDRESS?
RESTRICTED BREATHING? ANXIOUSNESS? TENSION? GUT ISSUES? CHEST/BODY PAINS? WITHDRAWN?

ON THE OTHER HAND, WHAT DID GO WELL TODAY?

WHAT CONTRIBUTED TO THINGS GOING WELL?

READ WHAT YOU WROTE ABOVE... WHAT DO YOU THINK YOU NEED TO #DoBetter ON PURPOSE TOMORROW?

MIND DUMP, PROCESS & UNRAVEL

If you have Accountability **YOU HAVE OWNERSHIP!**

MY DAILY NEWSLETTER
SELF REFLECTION = SELF AWARENESS

WHAT'S 1 THING IN THE *OUTSIDE* WORLD THAT AFFECTED ME TODAY?

WHAT ARE 1-2 THINGS I AM CONTENT WITH IN MY LIFE TODAY? THANKFUL? GRATEFUL?

WHAT 3 THINGS WENT ON TODAY IN *MY WORLD* THAT STOOD OUT? WHAT MADE AN IMPACT?

WHAT DIDN'T GO WELL TODAY?

HOW DID I FEEL EMOTIONALLY? WRITE THEM OUT

HOW DID YOU FEEL PHYSICALLY? WHAT DO I NEED TO ADDRESS?
RESTRICTED BREATHING? ANXIOUSNESS? TENSION? GUT ISSUES? CHEST/BODY PAINS? WITHDRAWN?

ON THE OTHER HAND, WHAT DID GO WELL TODAY?

WHAT CONTRIBUTED TO THINGS GOING WELL?

READ WHAT YOU WROTE ABOVE...WHAT DO YOU THINK YOU NEED TO #DoBetter ON PURPOSE TOMORROW?

MIND DUMP, PROCESS & UNRAVEL

If you have Accountability **YOU HAVE OWNERSHIP!**

MY DAILY NEWSLETTER
SELF REFLECTION = SELF AWARENESS

WHAT'S 1 THING IN THE *OUTSIDE* WORLD THAT AFFECTED ME TODAY?

WHAT ARE 1-2 THINGS I AM CONTENT WITH IN MY LIFE TODAY? THANKFUL? GRATEFUL?

WHAT 3 THINGS WENT ON TODAY IN *MY WORLD* THAT STOOD OUT? WHAT MADE AN IMPACT?

WHAT DIDN'T GO WELL TODAY?

HOW DID I FEEL EMOTIONALLY? WRITE THEM OUT

HOW DID YOU FEEL PHYSICALLY? WHAT DO I NEED TO ADDRESS?
RESTRICTED BREATHING? ANXIOUSNESS? TENSION? GUT ISSUES? CHEST/BODY PAINS? WITHDRAWN?

ON THE OTHER HAND, WHAT DID GO WELL TODAY?

WHAT CONTRIBUTED TO THINGS GOING WELL?

READ WHAT YOU WROTE ABOVE...WHAT DO YOU THINK YOU NEED TO #DoBetter ON PURPOSE TOMORROW?

MIND DUMP, PROCESS & UNRAVEL

If you have Accountability **YOU HAVE OWNERSHIP!**

MY DAILY NEWSLETTER
SELF REFLECTION = SELF AWARENESS

WHAT'S 1 THING IN THE *OUTSIDE* WORLD THAT AFFECTED ME TODAY?

WHAT ARE 1-2 THINGS I AM CONTENT WITH IN MY LIFE TODAY? THANKFUL? GRATEFUL?

WHAT 3 THINGS WENT ON TODAY IN *MY WORLD* THAT STOOD OUT? WHAT MADE AN IMPACT?

WHAT DIDN'T GO WELL TODAY?

HOW DID I FEEL EMOTIONALLY? WRITE THEM OUT

HOW DID YOU FEEL PHYSICALLY? WHAT DO I NEED TO ADDRESS?
RESTRICTED BREATHING? ANXIOUSNESS? TENSION? GUT ISSUES? CHEST/BODY PAINS? WITHDRAWN?

ON THE OTHER HAND, WHAT DID GO WELL TODAY?

WHAT CONTRIBUTED TO THINGS GOING WELL?

READ WHAT YOU WROTE ABOVE...WHAT DO YOU THINK YOU NEED TO #DoBetter ON PURPOSE TOMORROW?

MIND DUMP, PROCESS & UNRAVEL

If you take Responsibility
YOU HAVE OWNERSHIP!

ANSWER THESE QUESTIONS BELOW TO DEFINE YOUR PLAN FORWARD NEXT MONTH

WHERE DO YOU NEED TO DRAW A LINE TO #DOBETTER ON PURPOSE?

_____
_____
_____
_____
_____

WHAT HABIT DO YOU NEED TO WORK ON TO #DOBETTER ON PURPOSE?

_____
_____
_____

WHAT'S 1 EMOTION I WILL I FOCUS ON TO GET UNDER CONTROL?

WHAT WILL MOTIVATE YOU TO #DOBETTER ON PURPOSE?

_____
_____
_____
_____
_____
_____

WHAT NEEDS TO BE UNRAVELED ABOUT THIS PAST MONTH?

_____
_____
_____
_____
_____
_____

MIND DUMP, PROCESS & UNRAVEL

Self Awareness Alignment

Outline in these categories where you will *FOCUS* your self reflection
What things will you keep in the front of your mind?

RELATIONSHIPS

HEALTH

FINANCES

LESIURE

CAREER

SPIRITUALITY

GROWTH

NOTES:
_____
_____

Intentional Habits
HOW WILL YOU BE INTENTIONAL?

REMEBER THESE IN YOUR DAILY REFLECTIONS

MORNING HABITS	MID-DAY HABITS	EVENING HABITS

What **DISCIPLINES** will you put into place?

What will be your **WINNING STRATEGIE**S to change what you see on a daily basis?

Try: Prayer/meditation, written reminders, and accountability partners...

Write below 2-3 things you are willing to commit to doing to change behaviors (Think it, Speak it, Write it, Work it)

❯

❯

❯

If you have Accountability **YOU HAVE OWNERSHIP!**

MY DAILY NEWSLETTER
SELF REFLECTION = SELF AWARENESS

WHAT'S 1 THING IN THE *OUTSIDE* WORLD THAT AFFECTED ME TODAY?

WHAT ARE 1-2 THINGS I AM CONTENT WITH IN MY LIFE TODAY? THANKFUL? GRATEFUL?

WHAT 3 THINGS WENT ON TODAY IN *MY WORLD* THAT STOOD OUT? WHAT MADE AN IMPACT?

WHAT DIDN'T GO WELL TODAY?

HOW DID I FEEL EMOTIONALLY? WRITE THEM OUT

HOW DID YOU FEEL PHYSICALLY? WHAT DO I NEED TO ADDRESS?
RESTRICTED BREATHING? ANXIOUSNESS? TENSION? GUT ISSUES? CHEST/BODY PAINS? WITHDRAWN?

ON THE OTHER HAND, WHAT DID GO WELL TODAY?

WHAT CONTRIBUTED TO THINGS GOING WELL?

READ WHAT YOU WROTE ABOVE...WHAT DO YOU THINK YOU NEED TO #DoBetter ON PURPOSE TOMORROW?

MIND DUMP, PROCESS & UNRAVEL

If you have Accountability **YOU HAVE OWNERSHIP!**

MY DAILY NEWSLETTER
SELF REFLECTION = SELF AWARENESS

WHAT'S 1 THING IN THE *OUTSIDE* WORLD THAT AFFECTED ME TODAY?

WHAT ARE 1-2 THINGS I AM CONTENT WITH IN MY LIFE TODAY? THANKFUL? GRATEFUL?

WHAT 3 THINGS WENT ON TODAY IN *MY WORLD* THAT STOOD OUT? WHAT MADE AN IMPACT?

_____   _____   _____

WHAT DIDN'T GO WELL TODAY?

HOW DID I FEEL EMOTIONALLY? WRITE THEM OUT

— ————————————— +

HOW DID YOU FEEL PHYSICALLY? WHAT DO I NEED TO ADDRESS?
RESTRICTED BREATHING? ANXIOUSNESS? TENSION? GUT ISSUES? CHEST/BODY PAINS? WITHDRAWN?

ON THE OTHER HAND, WHAT DID GO WELL TODAY?

WHAT CONTRIBUTED TO THINGS GOING WELL?

READ WHAT YOU WROTE ABOVE...WHAT DO YOU THINK YOU NEED TO #DoBetter ON PURPOSE TOMORROW?

MIND DUMP, PROCESS & UNRAVEL

If you have Accountability **YOU HAVE OWNERSHIP!**

MY DAILY NEWSLETTER
SELF REFLECTION = SELF AWARENESS

WHAT'S 1 THING IN THE *OUTSIDE* WORLD THAT AFFECTED ME TODAY?

WHAT ARE 1-2 THINGS I AM CONTENT WITH IN MY LIFE TODAY? THANKFUL? GRATEFUL?

WHAT 3 THINGS WENT ON TODAY IN *MY WORLD* THAT STOOD OUT? WHAT MADE AN IMPACT?

WHAT DIDN'T GO WELL TODAY?

HOW DID I FEEL EMOTIONALLY? WRITE THEM OUT

HOW DID YOU FEEL PHYSICALLY? WHAT DO I NEED TO ADDRESS?
RESTRICTED BREATHING? ANXIOUSNESS? TENSION? GUT ISSUES? CHEST/BODY PAINS? WITHDRAWN?

ON THE OTHER HAND, WHAT DID GO WELL TODAY?

WHAT CONTRIBUTED TO THINGS GOING WELL?

READ WHAT YOU WROTE ABOVE... WHAT DO YOU THINK YOU NEED TO #DoBetter ON PURPOSE TOMORROW?

MIND DUMP, PROCESS & UNRAVEL

If you have Accountability **YOU HAVE OWNERSHIP!**

MY DAILY NEWSLETTER
SELF REFLECTION = SELF AWARENESS

WHAT'S 1 THING IN THE *OUTSIDE* WORLD THAT AFFECTED ME TODAY?

WHAT ARE 1-2 THINGS I AM CONTENT WITH IN MY LIFE TODAY? THANKFUL? GRATEFUL?

WHAT 3 THINGS WENT ON TODAY IN *MY WORLD* THAT STOOD OUT? WHAT MADE AN IMPACT?

WHAT DIDN'T GO WELL TODAY?

HOW DID I FEEL EMOTIONALLY? WRITE THEM OUT

HOW DID YOU FEEL PHYSICALLY? WHAT DO I NEED TO ADDRESS? RESTRICTED BREATHING? ANXIOUSNESS? TENSION? GUT ISSUES? CHEST/BODY PAINS? WITHDRAWN?

ON THE OTHER HAND, WHAT DID GO WELL TODAY?

WHAT CONTRIBUTED TO THINGS GOING WELL?

READ WHAT YOU WROTE ABOVE...WHAT DO YOU THINK YOU NEED TO #DoBetter ON PURPOSE TOMORROW?

MIND DUMP, PROCESS & UNRAVEL

If you have Accountability **YOU HAVE OWNERSHIP!**

MY DAILY NEWSLETTER
SELF REFLECTION = SELF AWARENESS

WHAT'S 1 THING IN THE *OUTSIDE* WORLD THAT AFFECTED ME TODAY?

WHAT ARE 1-2 THINGS I AM CONTENT WITH IN MY LIFE TODAY? THANKFUL? GRATEFUL?

WHAT 3 THINGS WENT ON TODAY IN *MY WORLD* THAT STOOD OUT? WHAT MADE AN IMPACT?

WHAT DIDN'T GO WELL TODAY?

HOW DID I FEEL EMOTIONALLY? WRITE THEM OUT

HOW DID YOU FEEL PHYSICALLY? WHAT DO I NEED TO ADDRESS?
RESTRICTED BREATHING? ANXIOUSNESS? TENSION? GUT ISSUES? CHEST/BODY PAINS? WITHDRAWN?

ON THE OTHER HAND, WHAT DID GO WELL TODAY?

WHAT CONTRIBUTED TO THINGS GOING WELL?

READ WHAT YOU WROTE ABOVE... WHAT DO YOU THINK YOU NEED TO #DoBetter ON PURPOSE TOMORROW?

MIND DUMP, PROCESS & UNRAVEL

If you have Accountability **YOU HAVE OWNERSHIP!**

MY DAILY NEWSLETTER
SELF REFLECTION = SELF AWARENESS

WHAT'S 1 THING IN THE *OUTSIDE* WORLD THAT AFFECTED ME TODAY?

WHAT ARE 1-2 THINGS I AM CONTENT WITH IN MY LIFE TODAY? THANKFUL? GRATEFUL?

WHAT 3 THINGS WENT ON TODAY IN *MY WORLD* THAT STOOD OUT? WHAT MADE AN IMPACT?

_____   _____   _____

WHAT DIDN'T GO WELL TODAY?

HOW DID I FEEL EMOTIONALLY? WRITE THEM OUT

HOW DID YOU FEEL PHYSICALLY? WHAT DO I NEED TO ADDRESS?
RESTRICTED BREATHING? ANXIOUSNESS? TENSION? GUT ISSUES? CHEST/BODY PAINS? WITHDRAWN?

ON THE OTHER HAND, WHAT DID GO WELL TODAY?

WHAT CONTRIBUTED TO THINGS GOING WELL?

READ WHAT YOU WROTE ABOVE…WHAT DO YOU THINK YOU NEED TO #DoBetter ON PURPOSE TOMORROW?

MIND DUMP, PROCESS & UNRAVEL

If you have Accountability **YOU HAVE OWNERSHIP!**

MY DAILY NEWSLETTER
SELF REFLECTION = SELF AWARENESS

WHAT'S 1 THING IN THE *OUTSIDE* WORLD THAT AFFECTED ME TODAY?

WHAT ARE 1-2 THINGS I AM CONTENT WITH IN MY LIFE TODAY? THANKFUL? GRATEFUL?

WHAT 3 THINGS WENT ON TODAY IN *MY WORLD* THAT STOOD OUT? WHAT MADE AN IMPACT?

WHAT DIDN'T GO WELL TODAY?

HOW DID I FEEL EMOTIONALLY? WRITE THEM OUT

HOW DID YOU FEEL PHYSICALLY? WHAT DO I NEED TO ADDRESS?
RESTRICTED BREATHING? ANXIOUSNESS? TENSION? GUT ISSUES? CHEST/BODY PAINS? WITHDRAWN?

ON THE OTHER HAND, WHAT DID GO WELL TODAY?

WHAT CONTRIBUTED TO THINGS GOING WELL?

READ WHAT YOU WROTE ABOVE…WHAT DO YOU THINK YOU NEED TO #DoBetter ON PURPOSE TOMORROW?

MIND DUMP, PROCESS & UNRAVEL

If you have Accountability **YOU HAVE OWNERSHIP!**

MY DAILY NEWSLETTER
SELF REFLECTION = SELF AWARENESS

WHAT'S 1 THING IN THE *OUTSIDE* WORLD THAT AFFECTED ME TODAY?

WHAT ARE 1-2 THINGS I AM CONTENT WITH IN MY LIFE TODAY? THANKFUL? GRATEFUL?

WHAT 3 THINGS WENT ON TODAY IN *MY WORLD* THAT STOOD OUT? WHAT MADE AN IMPACT?

_____   _____   _____

WHAT DIDN'T GO WELL TODAY?

HOW DID I FEEL EMOTIONALLY? WRITE THEM OUT

HOW DID YOU FEEL PHYSICALLY? WHAT DO I NEED TO ADDRESS?
RESTRICTED BREATHING? ANXIOUSNESS? TENSION? GUT ISSUES? CHEST/BODY PAINS? WITHDRAWN?

ON THE OTHER HAND, WHAT DID GO WELL TODAY?

WHAT CONTRIBUTED TO THINGS GOING WELL?

READ WHAT YOU WROTE ABOVE…WHAT DO YOU THINK YOU NEED TO #DoBetter ON PURPOSE TOMORROW?

MIND DUMP, PROCESS & UNRAVEL

If you have Accountability **YOU HAVE OWNERSHIP!**

MY DAILY NEWSLETTER
SELF REFLECTION = SELF AWARENESS

WHAT'S 1 THING IN THE *OUTSIDE* WORLD THAT AFFECTED ME TODAY?

WHAT ARE 1-2 THINGS I AM CONTENT WITH IN MY LIFE TODAY? THANKFUL? GRATEFUL?

WHAT 3 THINGS WENT ON TODAY IN *MY WORLD* THAT STOOD OUT? WHAT MADE AN IMPACT?

_____   _____   _____

WHAT DIDN'T GO WELL TODAY?

HOW DID I FEEL EMOTIONALLY? WRITE THEM OUT

HOW DID YOU FEEL PHYSICALLY? WHAT DO I NEED TO ADDRESS?
RESTRICTED BREATHING? ANXIOUSNESS? TENSION? GUT ISSUES? CHEST/BODY PAINS? WITHDRAWN?

ON THE OTHER HAND, WHAT DID GO WELL TODAY?

WHAT CONTRIBUTED TO THINGS GOING WELL?

READ WHAT YOU WROTE ABOVE… WHAT DO YOU THINK YOU NEED TO #DoBetter ON PURPOSE TOMORROW?

MIND DUMP, PROCESS & UNRAVEL

If you have Accountability **YOU HAVE OWNERSHIP!**

MY DAILY NEWSLETTER
SELF REFLECTION = SELF AWARENESS

What's 1 thing in the *OUTSIDE* world that Affected me today?

What are 1-2 things I am content with in my life today? Thankful? Grateful?

What 3 things went on today in *My World* that stood out? What made an impact?

_____   _____   _____

What didn't go well today?

_____
_____
_____
_____

How did I feel emotionally? Write them out

☹ 😕 😐 🙂 😊
— ═══════════ +

_____
_____
_____

How did you feel physically? What do I need to address? Restricted Breathing? Anxiousness? Tension? Gut issues? Chest/Body Pains? Withdrawn?

_____

On the other hand, What did go well today?

_____
_____
_____
_____
_____

What contributed to things going well?

_____
_____
_____
_____
_____

Read what you wrote above...What do you think you need to #DoBetter on Purpose Tomorrow?

_____
_____

MIND DUMP, PROCESS & UNRAVEL

If you have Accountability **YOU HAVE OWNERSHIP!**

MY DAILY NEWSLETTER
SELF REFLECTION = SELF AWARENESS

WHAT'S 1 THING IN THE *OUTSIDE* WORLD THAT AFFECTED ME TODAY?

WHAT ARE 1-2 THINGS I AM CONTENT WITH IN MY LIFE TODAY? THANKFUL? GRATEFUL?

WHAT 3 THINGS WENT ON TODAY IN *MY WORLD* THAT STOOD OUT? WHAT MADE AN IMPACT?

WHAT DIDN'T GO WELL TODAY?

HOW DID I FEEL EMOTIONALLY? WRITE THEM OUT

HOW DID YOU FEEL PHYSICALLY? WHAT DO I NEED TO ADDRESS?
RESTRICTED BREATHING? ANXIOUSNESS? TENSION? GUT ISSUES? CHEST/BODY PAINS? WITHDRAWN?

ON THE OTHER HAND, WHAT DID GO WELL TODAY?

WHAT CONTRIBUTED TO THINGS GOING WELL?

READ WHAT YOU WROTE ABOVE... WHAT DO YOU THINK YOU NEED TO #DoBetter ON PURPOSE TOMORROW?

MIND DUMP, PROCESS & UNRAVEL

If you have Accountability **YOU HAVE OWNERSHIP!**

MY DAILY NEWSLETTER
SELF REFLECTION = SELF AWARENESS

WHAT'S 1 THING IN THE *OUTSIDE* WORLD THAT AFFECTED ME TODAY?

WHAT ARE 1-2 THINGS I AM CONTENT WITH IN MY LIFE TODAY? THANKFUL? GRATEFUL?

WHAT 3 THINGS WENT ON TODAY IN *MY WORLD* THAT STOOD OUT? WHAT MADE AN IMPACT?

WHAT DIDN'T GO WELL TODAY?

HOW DID I FEEL EMOTIONALLY? WRITE THEM OUT

HOW DID YOU FEEL PHYSICALLY? WHAT DO I NEED TO ADDRESS? RESTRICTED BREATHING? ANXIOUSNESS? TENSION? GUT ISSUES? CHEST/BODY PAINS? WITHDRAWN?

ON THE OTHER HAND, WHAT DID GO WELL TODAY?

WHAT CONTRIBUTED TO THINGS GOING WELL?

READ WHAT YOU WROTE ABOVE...WHAT DO YOU THINK YOU NEED TO #DoBetter ON PURPOSE TOMORROW?

MIND DUMP, PROCESS & UNRAVEL

If you have Accountability **YOU HAVE OWNERSHIP!**

MY DAILY NEWSLETTER
SELF REFLECTION = SELF AWARENESS

WHAT'S 1 THING IN THE *OUTSIDE* WORLD THAT AFFECTED ME TODAY?

WHAT ARE 1-2 THINGS I AM CONTENT WITH IN MY LIFE TODAY? THANKFUL? GRATEFUL?

WHAT 3 THINGS WENT ON TODAY IN *MY WORLD* THAT STOOD OUT? WHAT MADE AN IMPACT?

WHAT DIDN'T GO WELL TODAY?

HOW DID I FEEL EMOTIONALLY? WRITE THEM OUT

HOW DID YOU FEEL PHYSICALLY? WHAT DO I NEED TO ADDRESS?
RESTRICTED BREATHING? ANXIOUSNESS? TENSION? GUT ISSUES? CHEST/BODY PAINS? WITHDRAWN?

ON THE OTHER HAND, WHAT DID GO WELL TODAY?

WHAT CONTRIBUTED TO THINGS GOING WELL?

READ WHAT YOU WROTE ABOVE... WHAT DO YOU THINK YOU NEED TO #DoBetter ON PURPOSE TOMORROW?

MIND DUMP, PROCESS & UNRAVEL

If you have Accountability **YOU HAVE OWNERSHIP!**

MY DAILY NEWSLETTER
SELF REFLECTION = SELF AWARENESS

WHAT'S 1 THING IN THE *OUTSIDE* WORLD THAT AFFECTED ME TODAY?

WHAT ARE 1-2 THINGS I AM CONTENT WITH IN MY LIFE TODAY? THANKFUL? GRATEFUL?

WHAT 3 THINGS WENT ON TODAY IN *MY WORLD* THAT STOOD OUT? WHAT MADE AN IMPACT?

_____   _____   _____

WHAT DIDN'T GO WELL TODAY?

_____
_____
_____
_____

HOW DID I FEEL EMOTIONALLY? WRITE THEM OUT

– ———————— +

_____
_____
_____
_____

HOW DID YOU FEEL PHYSICALLY? WHAT DO I NEED TO ADDRESS?
RESTRICTED BREATHING? ANXIOUSNESS? TENSION? GUT ISSUES? CHEST/BODY PAINS? WITHDRAWN?

_____

ON THE OTHER HAND, WHAT DID GO WELL TODAY?

_____
_____
_____
_____
_____

WHAT CONTRIBUTED TO THINGS GOING WELL?

_____
_____
_____
_____
_____

READ WHAT YOU WROTE ABOVE…WHAT DO YOU THINK YOU NEED TO #DoBetter ON PURPOSE TOMORROW?

_____
_____

MIND DUMP, PROCESS & UNRAVEL

If you have Accountability **YOU HAVE OWNERSHIP!**

MY DAILY NEWSLETTER
SELF REFLECTION = SELF AWARENESS

WHAT'S 1 THING IN THE *OUTSIDE* WORLD THAT AFFECTED ME TODAY?

WHAT ARE 1-2 THINGS I AM CONTENT WITH IN MY LIFE TODAY? THANKFUL? GRATEFUL?

WHAT 3 THINGS WENT ON TODAY IN *MY WORLD* THAT STOOD OUT? WHAT MADE AN IMPACT?

_____ _____ _____

WHAT DIDN'T GO WELL TODAY?

_____
_____
_____
_____

HOW DID I FEEL EMOTIONALLY? WRITE THEM OUT

_____
_____
_____
_____

HOW DID YOU FEEL PHYSICALLY? WHAT DO I NEED TO ADDRESS?
RESTRICTED BREATHING? ANXIOUSNESS? TENSION? GUT ISSUES? CHEST/BODY PAINS? WITHDRAWN?

_____

ON THE OTHER HAND, WHAT DID GO WELL TODAY?

_____
_____
_____
_____
_____

WHAT CONTRIBUTED TO THINGS GOING WELL?

_____
_____
_____
_____
_____

READ WHAT YOU WROTE ABOVE…WHAT DO YOU THINK YOU NEED TO #DoBetter ON PURPOSE TOMORROW?

_____
_____

MIND DUMP, PROCESS & UNRAVEL

If you have Accountability **YOU HAVE OWNERSHIP!**

MY DAILY NEWSLETTER
SELF REFLECTION = SELF AWARENESS

WHAT'S 1 THING IN THE *OUTSIDE* WORLD THAT AFFECTED ME TODAY?

WHAT ARE 1-2 THINGS I AM CONTENT WITH IN MY LIFE TODAY? THANKFUL? GRATEFUL?

WHAT 3 THINGS WENT ON TODAY IN *MY WORLD* THAT STOOD OUT? WHAT MADE AN IMPACT?

_____ _____ _____

WHAT DIDN'T GO WELL TODAY?

HOW DID I FEEL EMOTIONALLY? WRITE THEM OUT

HOW DID YOU FEEL PHYSICALLY? WHAT DO I NEED TO ADDRESS?
RESTRICTED BREATHING? ANXIOUSNESS? TENSION? GUT ISSUES? CHEST/BODY PAINS? WITHDRAWN?

ON THE OTHER HAND, WHAT DID GO WELL TODAY?

WHAT CONTRIBUTED TO THINGS GOING WELL?

READ WHAT YOU WROTE ABOVE...WHAT DO YOU THINK YOU NEED TO #DoBetter ON PURPOSE TOMORROW?

MIND DUMP, PROCESS & UNRAVEL

If you have Accountability **YOU HAVE OWNERSHIP!**

MY DAILY NEWSLETTER
SELF REFLECTION = SELF AWARENESS

WHAT'S 1 THING IN THE *OUTSIDE* WORLD THAT AFFECTED ME TODAY?

WHAT ARE 1-2 THINGS I AM CONTENT WITH IN MY LIFE TODAY? THANKFUL? GRATEFUL?

WHAT 3 THINGS WENT ON TODAY IN *MY WORLD* THAT STOOD OUT? WHAT MADE AN IMPACT?

WHAT DIDN'T GO WELL TODAY?

HOW DID I FEEL EMOTIONALLY? WRITE THEM OUT

HOW DID YOU FEEL PHYSICALLY? WHAT DO I NEED TO ADDRESS?
RESTRICTED BREATHING? ANXIOUSNESS? TENSION? GUT ISSUES? CHEST/BODY PAINS? WITHDRAWN?

ON THE OTHER HAND, WHAT DID GO WELL TODAY?

WHAT CONTRIBUTED TO THINGS GOING WELL?

READ WHAT YOU WROTE ABOVE…WHAT DO YOU THINK YOU NEED TO #DOBETTER ON PURPOSE TOMORROW?

MIND DUMP, PROCESS & UNRAVEL

If you have Accountability **YOU HAVE OWNERSHIP!**

MY DAILY NEWSLETTER
SELF REFLECTION = SELF AWARENESS

WHAT'S 1 THING IN THE *OUTSIDE* WORLD THAT AFFECTED ME TODAY?

WHAT ARE 1-2 THINGS I AM CONTENT WITH IN MY LIFE TODAY? THANKFUL? GRATEFUL?

WHAT 3 THINGS WENT ON TODAY IN *MY WORLD* THAT STOOD OUT? WHAT MADE AN IMPACT?

WHAT DIDN'T GO WELL TODAY?

HOW DID I FEEL EMOTIONALLY? WRITE THEM OUT

HOW DID YOU FEEL PHYSICALLY? WHAT DO I NEED TO ADDRESS?
RESTRICTED BREATHING? ANXIOUSNESS? TENSION? GUT ISSUES? CHEST/BODY PAINS? WITHDRAWN?

ON THE OTHER HAND, WHAT DID GO WELL TODAY?

WHAT CONTRIBUTED TO THINGS GOING WELL?

READ WHAT YOU WROTE ABOVE...WHAT DO YOU THINK YOU NEED TO #DoBetter ON PURPOSE TOMORROW?

MIND DUMP, PROCESS & UNRAVEL

If you have Accountability **YOU HAVE OWNERSHIP!**

MY DAILY NEWSLETTER
SELF REFLECTION = SELF AWARENESS

WHAT'S 1 THING IN THE *OUTSIDE* WORLD THAT AFFECTED ME TODAY?

WHAT ARE 1-2 THINGS I AM CONTENT WITH IN MY LIFE TODAY? THANKFUL? GRATEFUL?

WHAT 3 THINGS WENT ON TODAY IN *MY WORLD* THAT STOOD OUT? WHAT MADE AN IMPACT?

WHAT DIDN'T GO WELL TODAY?

HOW DID I FEEL EMOTIONALLY? WRITE THEM OUT

HOW DID YOU FEEL PHYSICALLY? WHAT DO I NEED TO ADDRESS?
RESTRICTED BREATHING? ANXIOUSNESS? TENSION? GUT ISSUES? CHEST/BODY PAINS? WITHDRAWN?

ON THE OTHER HAND, WHAT DID GO WELL TODAY?

WHAT CONTRIBUTED TO THINGS GOING WELL?

READ WHAT YOU WROTE ABOVE...WHAT DO YOU THINK YOU NEED TO #DoBetter ON PURPOSE TOMORROW?

MIND DUMP, PROCESS & UNRAVEL

If you have Accountability **YOU HAVE OWNERSHIP!**

MY DAILY NEWSLETTER
SELF REFLECTION = SELF AWARENESS

WHAT'S 1 THING IN THE *OUTSIDE* WORLD THAT AFFECTED ME TODAY?

WHAT ARE 1-2 THINGS I AM CONTENT WITH IN MY LIFE TODAY? THANKFUL? GRATEFUL?

WHAT 3 THINGS WENT ON TODAY IN *MY WORLD* THAT STOOD OUT? WHAT MADE AN IMPACT?

WHAT DIDN'T GO WELL TODAY?

HOW DID I FEEL EMOTIONALLY? WRITE THEM OUT

HOW DID YOU FEEL PHYSICALLY? WHAT DO I NEED TO ADDRESS?
RESTRICTED BREATHING? ANXIOUSNESS? TENSION? GUT ISSUES? CHEST/BODY PAINS? WITHDRAWN?

ON THE OTHER HAND, WHAT DID GO WELL TODAY?

WHAT CONTRIBUTED TO THINGS GOING WELL?

READ WHAT YOU WROTE ABOVE...WHAT DO YOU THINK YOU NEED TO #DoBetter ON PURPOSE TOMORROW?

MIND DUMP, PROCESS & UNRAVEL

If you have Accountability **YOU HAVE OWNERSHIP!**

MY DAILY NEWSLETTER
SELF REFLECTION = SELF AWARENESS

WHAT'S 1 THING IN THE *OUTSIDE* WORLD THAT AFFECTED ME TODAY?

WHAT ARE 1-2 THINGS I AM CONTENT WITH IN MY LIFE TODAY? THANKFUL? GRATEFUL?

WHAT 3 THINGS WENT ON TODAY IN *MY WORLD* THAT STOOD OUT? WHAT MADE AN IMPACT?

WHAT DIDN'T GO WELL TODAY?

HOW DID I FEEL EMOTIONALLY? WRITE THEM OUT

HOW DID YOU FEEL PHYSICALLY? WHAT DO I NEED TO ADDRESS?
RESTRICTED BREATHING? ANXIOUSNESS? TENSION? GUT ISSUES? CHEST/BODY PAINS? WITHDRAWN?

ON THE OTHER HAND, WHAT DID GO WELL TODAY?

WHAT CONTRIBUTED TO THINGS GOING WELL?

READ WHAT YOU WROTE ABOVE…WHAT DO YOU THINK YOU NEED TO #DoBetter ON PURPOSE TOMORROW?

MIND DUMP, PROCESS & UNRAVEL

If you have Accountability **YOU HAVE OWNERSHIP!**

MY DAILY NEWSLETTER
SELF REFLECTION = SELF AWARENESS

WHAT'S 1 THING IN THE *OUTSIDE* WORLD THAT AFFECTED ME TODAY?

WHAT ARE 1-2 THINGS I AM CONTENT WITH IN MY LIFE TODAY? THANKFUL? GRATEFUL?

WHAT 3 THINGS WENT ON TODAY IN *MY WORLD* THAT STOOD OUT? WHAT MADE AN IMPACT?

WHAT DIDN'T GO WELL TODAY?

HOW DID I FEEL EMOTIONALLY? WRITE THEM OUT

HOW DID YOU FEEL PHYSICALLY? WHAT DO I NEED TO ADDRESS?
RESTRICTED BREATHING? ANXIOUSNESS? TENSION? GUT ISSUES? CHEST/BODY PAINS? WITHDRAWN?

ON THE OTHER HAND, WHAT DID GO WELL TODAY?

WHAT CONTRIBUTED TO THINGS GOING WELL?

READ WHAT YOU WROTE ABOVE...WHAT DO YOU THINK YOU NEED TO #DoBetter ON PURPOSE TOMORROW?

MIND DUMP, PROCESS & UNRAVEL

If you have Accountability **YOU HAVE OWNERSHIP!**

MY DAILY NEWSLETTER
SELF REFLECTION = SELF AWARENESS

WHAT'S 1 THING IN THE *OUTSIDE* WORLD THAT AFFECTED ME TODAY?

WHAT ARE 1-2 THINGS I AM CONTENT WITH IN MY LIFE TODAY? THANKFUL? GRATEFUL?

WHAT 3 THINGS WENT ON TODAY IN *MY WORLD* THAT STOOD OUT? WHAT MADE AN IMPACT?

WHAT DIDN'T GO WELL TODAY?

HOW DID I FEEL EMOTIONALLY? WRITE THEM OUT

— ————————————— +

HOW DID YOU FEEL PHYSICALLY? WHAT DO I NEED TO ADDRESS?
RESTRICTED BREATHING? ANXIOUSNESS? TENSION? GUT ISSUES? CHEST/BODY PAINS? WITHDRAWN?

ON THE OTHER HAND, WHAT DID GO WELL TODAY?

WHAT CONTRIBUTED TO THINGS GOING WELL?

READ WHAT YOU WROTE ABOVE...WHAT DO YOU THINK YOU NEED TO #DoBetter ON PURPOSE TOMORROW?

MIND DUMP, PROCESS & UNRAVEL

If you have Accountability **YOU HAVE OWNERSHIP!**

MY DAILY NEWSLETTER
SELF REFLECTION = SELF AWARENESS

WHAT'S 1 THING IN THE *OUTSIDE* WORLD THAT AFFECTED ME TODAY?

WHAT ARE 1-2 THINGS I AM CONTENT WITH IN MY LIFE TODAY? THANKFUL? GRATEFUL?

WHAT 3 THINGS WENT ON TODAY IN *MY WORLD* THAT STOOD OUT? WHAT MADE AN IMPACT?

WHAT DIDN'T GO WELL TODAY?

HOW DID I FEEL EMOTIONALLY? WRITE THEM OUT

HOW DID YOU FEEL PHYSICALLY? WHAT DO I NEED TO ADDRESS?
RESTRICTED BREATHING? ANXIOUSNESS? TENSION? GUT ISSUES? CHEST/BODY PAINS? WITHDRAWN?

ON THE OTHER HAND, WHAT DID GO WELL TODAY?

WHAT CONTRIBUTED TO THINGS GOING WELL?

READ WHAT YOU WROTE ABOVE...WHAT DO YOU THINK YOU NEED TO #DoBetter ON PURPOSE TOMORROW?

MIND DUMP, PROCESS & UNRAVEL

If you have Accountability **YOU HAVE OWNERSHIP!**

MY DAILY NEWSLETTER
SELF REFLECTION = SELF AWARENESS

WHAT'S 1 THING IN THE *OUTSIDE* WORLD THAT AFFECTED ME TODAY?

WHAT ARE 1-2 THINGS I AM CONTENT WITH IN MY LIFE TODAY? THANKFUL? GRATEFUL?

WHAT 3 THINGS WENT ON TODAY IN *MY WORLD* THAT STOOD OUT? WHAT MADE AN IMPACT?

WHAT DIDN'T GO WELL TODAY?

HOW DID I FEEL EMOTIONALLY? WRITE THEM OUT

HOW DID YOU FEEL PHYSICALLY? WHAT DO I NEED TO ADDRESS?
RESTRICTED BREATHING? ANXIOUSNESS? TENSION? GUT ISSUES? CHEST/BODY PAINS? WITHDRAWN?

ON THE OTHER HAND, WHAT DID GO WELL TODAY?

WHAT CONTRIBUTED TO THINGS GOING WELL?

READ WHAT YOU WROTE ABOVE…WHAT DO YOU THINK YOU NEED TO #DoBetter ON PURPOSE TOMORROW?

MIND DUMP, PROCESS & UNRAVEL

If you have Accountability **YOU HAVE OWNERSHIP!**

MY DAILY NEWSLETTER
SELF REFLECTION = SELF AWARENESS

WHAT'S 1 THING IN THE *OUTSIDE* WORLD THAT AFFECTED ME TODAY?

WHAT ARE 1-2 THINGS I AM CONTENT WITH IN MY LIFE TODAY? THANKFUL? GRATEFUL?

WHAT 3 THINGS WENT ON TODAY IN *MY WORLD* THAT STOOD OUT? WHAT MADE AN IMPACT?

_____ _____ _____

WHAT DIDN'T GO WELL TODAY?

HOW DID I FEEL EMOTIONALLY? WRITE THEM OUT

HOW DID YOU FEEL PHYSICALLY? WHAT DO I NEED TO ADDRESS?
RESTRICTED BREATHING? ANXIOUSNESS? TENSION? GUT ISSUES? CHEST/BODY PAINS? WITHDRAWN?

ON THE OTHER HAND, WHAT DID GO WELL TODAY?

WHAT CONTRIBUTED TO THINGS GOING WELL?

READ WHAT YOU WROTE ABOVE…WHAT DO YOU THINK YOU NEED TO #DoBetter ON PURPOSE TOMORROW?

MIND DUMP, PROCESS & UNRAVEL

If you have Accountability **YOU HAVE OWNERSHIP!**

MY DAILY NEWSLETTER
SELF REFLECTION = SELF AWARENESS

WHAT'S 1 THING IN THE *OUTSIDE* WORLD THAT AFFECTED ME TODAY?

WHAT ARE 1-2 THINGS I AM CONTENT WITH IN MY LIFE TODAY? THANKFUL? GRATEFUL?

WHAT 3 THINGS WENT ON TODAY IN *MY WORLD* THAT STOOD OUT? WHAT MADE AN IMPACT?

WHAT DIDN'T GO WELL TODAY?

HOW DID I FEEL EMOTIONALLY? WRITE THEM OUT

HOW DID YOU FEEL PHYSICALLY? WHAT DO I NEED TO ADDRESS?
RESTRICTED BREATHING? ANXIOUSNESS? TENSION? GUT ISSUES? CHEST/BODY PAINS? WITHDRAWN?

ON THE OTHER HAND, WHAT DID GO WELL TODAY?

WHAT CONTRIBUTED TO THINGS GOING WELL?

READ WHAT YOU WROTE ABOVE… WHAT DO YOU THINK YOU NEED TO #DoBetter ON PURPOSE TOMORROW?

MIND DUMP, PROCESS & UNRAVEL

If you have Accountability **YOU HAVE OWNERSHIP!**

MY DAILY NEWSLETTER
SELF REFLECTION = SELF AWARENESS

WHAT'S 1 THING IN THE *OUTSIDE* WORLD THAT AFFECTED ME TODAY?

WHAT ARE 1-2 THINGS I AM CONTENT WITH IN MY LIFE TODAY? THANKFUL? GRATEFUL?

WHAT 3 THINGS WENT ON TODAY IN *MY WORLD* THAT STOOD OUT? WHAT MADE AN IMPACT?

WHAT DIDN'T GO WELL TODAY?

HOW DID I FEEL EMOTIONALLY? WRITE THEM OUT

HOW DID YOU FEEL PHYSICALLY? WHAT DO I NEED TO ADDRESS? RESTRICTED BREATHING? ANXIOUSNESS? TENSION? GUT ISSUES? CHEST/BODY PAINS? WITHDRAWN?

ON THE OTHER HAND, WHAT DID GO WELL TODAY?

WHAT CONTRIBUTED TO THINGS GOING WELL?

READ WHAT YOU WROTE ABOVE...WHAT DO YOU THINK YOU NEED TO #DoBetter ON PURPOSE TOMORROW?

MIND DUMP, PROCESS & UNRAVEL

If you have Accountability **YOU HAVE OWNERSHIP!**

MY DAILY NEWSLETTER
SELF REFLECTION = SELF AWARENESS

WHAT'S 1 THING IN THE *OUTSIDE* WORLD THAT AFFECTED ME TODAY?

WHAT ARE 1-2 THINGS I AM CONTENT WITH IN MY LIFE TODAY? THANKFUL? GRATEFUL?

WHAT 3 THINGS WENT ON TODAY IN *MY WORLD* THAT STOOD OUT? WHAT MADE AN IMPACT?

_____   _____   _____

WHAT DIDN'T GO WELL TODAY?

_____
_____
_____
_____

HOW DID I FEEL EMOTIONALLY? WRITE THEM OUT

☹ 🙁 😐 🙂 😊
— _____ +

_____
_____
_____
_____

HOW DID YOU FEEL PHYSICALLY? WHAT DO I NEED TO ADDRESS?
RESTRICTED BREATHING? ANXIOUSNESS? TENSION? GUT ISSUES? CHEST/BODY PAINS? WITHDRAWN?

_____

ON THE OTHER HAND, WHAT DID GO WELL TODAY?

_____
_____
_____
_____
_____

WHAT CONTRIBUTED TO THINGS GOING WELL?

_____
_____
_____
_____
_____

READ WHAT YOU WROTE ABOVE... WHAT DO YOU THINK YOU NEED TO #DoBetter ON PURPOSE TOMORROW?

_____
_____

MIND DUMP, PROCESS & UNRAVEL

If you have Accountability **YOU HAVE OWNERSHIP!**

MY DAILY NEWSLETTER
SELF REFLECTION = SELF AWARENESS

WHAT'S 1 THING IN THE *OUTSIDE* WORLD THAT AFFECTED ME TODAY?

WHAT ARE 1-2 THINGS I AM CONTENT WITH IN MY LIFE TODAY? THANKFUL? GRATEFUL?

WHAT 3 THINGS WENT ON TODAY IN *MY WORLD* THAT STOOD OUT? WHAT MADE AN IMPACT?

_____   _____   _____

WHAT DIDN'T GO WELL TODAY?

HOW DID I FEEL EMOTIONALLY? WRITE THEM OUT

HOW DID YOU FEEL PHYSICALLY? WHAT DO I NEED TO ADDRESS?
RESTRICTED BREATHING? ANXIOUSNESS? TENSION? GUT ISSUES? CHEST/BODY PAINS? WITHDRAWN?

ON THE OTHER HAND, WHAT DID GO WELL TODAY?

WHAT CONTRIBUTED TO THINGS GOING WELL?

READ WHAT YOU WROTE ABOVE...WHAT DO YOU THINK YOU NEED TO #DoBetter ON PURPOSE TOMORROW?

MIND DUMP, PROCESS & UNRAVEL

If you have Accountability **YOU HAVE OWNERSHIP!**

MY DAILY NEWSLETTER
SELF REFLECTION = SELF AWARENESS

WHAT'S 1 THING IN THE *OUTSIDE* WORLD THAT AFFECTED ME TODAY?

WHAT ARE 1-2 THINGS I AM CONTENT WITH IN MY LIFE TODAY? THANKFUL? GRATEFUL?

WHAT 3 THINGS WENT ON TODAY IN *MY WORLD* THAT STOOD OUT? WHAT MADE AN IMPACT?

WHAT DIDN'T GO WELL TODAY?

HOW DID I FEEL EMOTIONALLY? WRITE THEM OUT

HOW DID YOU FEEL PHYSICALLY? WHAT DO I NEED TO ADDRESS?
RESTRICTED BREATHING? ANXIOUSNESS? TENSION? GUT ISSUES? CHEST/BODY PAINS? WITHDRAWN?

ON THE OTHER HAND, WHAT DID GO WELL TODAY?

WHAT CONTRIBUTED TO THINGS GOING WELL?

READ WHAT YOU WROTE ABOVE...WHAT DO YOU THINK YOU NEED TO #DoBetter ON PURPOSE TOMORROW?

MIND DUMP, PROCESS & UNRAVEL

If you take Responsibility
YOU HAVE OWNERSHIP!
ANSWER THESE QUESTIONS BELOW TO DEFINE YOUR PLAN FORWARD NEXT MONTH

WHERE DO YOU NEED TO DRAW A LINE TO #DOBETTER ON PURPOSE?

_____
_____
_____
_____
_____

WHAT HABIT DO YOU NEED TO WORK ON TO #DOBETTER ON PURPOSE?

_____
_____

WHAT'S 1 EMOTION I WILL I FOCUS ON TO GET UNDER CONTROL?

WHAT WILL MOTIVATE YOU TO #DOBETTER ON PURPOSE?

_____
_____
_____
_____
_____
_____

WHAT NEEDS TO BE UNRAVELED ABOUT THIS PAST MONTH?

_____
_____
_____
_____
_____
_____

MIND DUMP, PROCESS & UNRAVEL

Self Awareness Alignment

OUTLINE IN THESE CATEGORIES WHERE YOU WILL *FOCUS* YOUR SELF REFLECTION
WHAT THINGS WILL YOU KEEP IN THE FRONT OF YOUR MIND?

RELATIONSHIPS

HEALTH

FINANCES

LESIURE

CAREER

SPIRITUALITY

GROWTH

NOTES:
_____
_____

Intentional Habits
HOW WILL YOU BE INTENTIONAL?

REMEBER THESE IN YOUR DAILY REFLECTIONS

MORNING HABITS	MID-DAY HABITS	EVENING HABITS

What **DISCIPLINES** will you put into place?

What will be your **WINNING STRATEGIE**S to change what you see on a daily basis?

Try: Prayer/meditation, written reminders, and accountability partners...

Write below 2-3 things you are willing to commit to doing to change behaviors (Think it, Speak it, Write it, Work it)

➤

➤

➤

If you have Accountability **YOU HAVE OWNERSHIP!**

MY DAILY NEWSLETTER
SELF REFLECTION = SELF AWARENESS

WHAT'S 1 THING IN THE *OUTSIDE* WORLD THAT AFFECTED ME TODAY?

WHAT ARE 1-2 THINGS I AM CONTENT WITH IN MY LIFE TODAY? THANKFUL? GRATEFUL?

WHAT 3 THINGS WENT ON TODAY IN *MY WORLD* THAT STOOD OUT? WHAT MADE AN IMPACT?

WHAT DIDN'T GO WELL TODAY?

HOW DID I FEEL EMOTIONALLY? WRITE THEM OUT

HOW DID YOU FEEL PHYSICALLY? WHAT DO I NEED TO ADDRESS?
RESTRICTED BREATHING? ANXIOUSNESS? TENSION? GUT ISSUES? CHEST/BODY PAINS? WITHDRAWN?

ON THE OTHER HAND, WHAT DID GO WELL TODAY?

WHAT CONTRIBUTED TO THINGS GOING WELL?

READ WHAT YOU WROTE ABOVE...WHAT DO YOU THINK YOU NEED TO #DoBetter ON PURPOSE TOMORROW?

MIND DUMP, PROCESS & UNRAVEL

If you have Accountability **YOU HAVE OWNERSHIP!**

MY DAILY NEWSLETTER
SELF REFLECTION = SELF AWARENESS

WHAT'S 1 THING IN THE *OUTSIDE* WORLD THAT AFFECTED ME TODAY?

WHAT ARE 1-2 THINGS I AM CONTENT WITH IN MY LIFE TODAY? THANKFUL? GRATEFUL?

WHAT 3 THINGS WENT ON TODAY IN *MY WORLD* THAT STOOD OUT? WHAT MADE AN IMPACT?

WHAT DIDN'T GO WELL TODAY?

HOW DID I FEEL EMOTIONALLY? WRITE THEM OUT

HOW DID YOU FEEL PHYSICALLY? WHAT DO I NEED TO ADDRESS?
RESTRICTED BREATHING? ANXIOUSNESS? TENSION? GUT ISSUES? CHEST/BODY PAINS? WITHDRAWN?

ON THE OTHER HAND, WHAT DID GO WELL TODAY?

WHAT CONTRIBUTED TO THINGS GOING WELL?

READ WHAT YOU WROTE ABOVE... WHAT DO YOU THINK YOU NEED TO #DoBetter ON PURPOSE TOMORROW?

MIND DUMP, PROCESS & UNRAVEL

If you have Accountability **YOU HAVE OWNERSHIP!**

MY DAILY NEWSLETTER
SELF REFLECTION = SELF AWARENESS

WHAT'S 1 THING IN THE *OUTSIDE* WORLD THAT AFFECTED ME TODAY?

WHAT ARE 1-2 THINGS I AM CONTENT WITH IN MY LIFE TODAY? THANKFUL? GRATEFUL?

WHAT 3 THINGS WENT ON TODAY IN *MY WORLD* THAT STOOD OUT? WHAT MADE AN IMPACT?

WHAT DIDN'T GO WELL TODAY?

HOW DID I FEEL EMOTIONALLY? WRITE THEM OUT

HOW DID YOU FEEL PHYSICALLY? WHAT DO I NEED TO ADDRESS?
RESTRICTED BREATHING? ANXIOUSNESS? TENSION? GUT ISSUES? CHEST/BODY PAINS? WITHDRAWN?

ON THE OTHER HAND, WHAT DID GO WELL TODAY?

WHAT CONTRIBUTED TO THINGS GOING WELL?

READ WHAT YOU WROTE ABOVE...WHAT DO YOU THINK YOU NEED TO #DoBetter ON PURPOSE TOMORROW?

MIND DUMP, PROCESS & UNRAVEL

If you have Accountability **YOU HAVE OWNERSHIP!**

MY DAILY NEWSLETTER
SELF REFLECTION = SELF AWARENESS

WHAT'S 1 THING IN THE *OUTSIDE* WORLD THAT AFFECTED ME TODAY?

WHAT ARE 1-2 THINGS I AM CONTENT WITH IN MY LIFE TODAY? THANKFUL? GRATEFUL?

WHAT 3 THINGS WENT ON TODAY IN *MY WORLD* THAT STOOD OUT? WHAT MADE AN IMPACT?

WHAT DIDN'T GO WELL TODAY?

HOW DID I FEEL EMOTIONALLY? WRITE THEM OUT

HOW DID YOU FEEL PHYSICALLY? WHAT DO I NEED TO ADDRESS?
RESTRICTED BREATHING? ANXIOUSNESS? TENSION? GUT ISSUES? CHEST/BODY PAINS? WITHDRAWN?

ON THE OTHER HAND, WHAT DID GO WELL TODAY?

WHAT CONTRIBUTED TO THINGS GOING WELL?

READ WHAT YOU WROTE ABOVE...WHAT DO YOU THINK YOU NEED TO #DoBetter ON PURPOSE TOMORROW?

MIND DUMP, PROCESS & UNRAVEL

If you have Accountability **YOU HAVE OWNERSHIP!**

MY DAILY NEWSLETTER
SELF REFLECTION = SELF AWARENESS

WHAT'S 1 THING IN THE *OUTSIDE* WORLD THAT AFFECTED ME TODAY?

WHAT ARE 1-2 THINGS I AM CONTENT WITH IN MY LIFE TODAY? THANKFUL? GRATEFUL?

WHAT 3 THINGS WENT ON TODAY IN *MY WORLD* THAT STOOD OUT? WHAT MADE AN IMPACT?

WHAT DIDN'T GO WELL TODAY?

HOW DID I FEEL EMOTIONALLY? WRITE THEM OUT

HOW DID YOU FEEL PHYSICALLY? WHAT DO I NEED TO ADDRESS?
RESTRICTED BREATHING? ANXIOUSNESS? TENSION? GUT ISSUES? CHEST/BODY PAINS? WITHDRAWN?

ON THE OTHER HAND, WHAT DID GO WELL TODAY?

WHAT CONTRIBUTED TO THINGS GOING WELL?

READ WHAT YOU WROTE ABOVE...WHAT DO YOU THINK YOU NEED TO #DoBetter ON PURPOSE TOMORROW?

MIND DUMP, PROCESS & UNRAVEL

If you have Accountability **YOU HAVE OWNERSHIP!**

MY DAILY NEWSLETTER
SELF REFLECTION = SELF AWARENESS

WHAT'S 1 THING IN THE *OUTSIDE* WORLD THAT AFFECTED ME TODAY?

WHAT ARE 1-2 THINGS I AM CONTENT WITH IN MY LIFE TODAY? THANKFUL? GRATEFUL?

WHAT 3 THINGS WENT ON TODAY IN *MY WORLD* THAT STOOD OUT? WHAT MADE AN IMPACT?

WHAT DIDN'T GO WELL TODAY?

HOW DID I FEEL EMOTIONALLY? WRITE THEM OUT

HOW DID YOU FEEL PHYSICALLY? WHAT DO I NEED TO ADDRESS?
RESTRICTED BREATHING? ANXIOUSNESS? TENSION? GUT ISSUES? CHEST/BODY PAINS? WITHDRAWN?

ON THE OTHER HAND, WHAT DID GO WELL TODAY?

WHAT CONTRIBUTED TO THINGS GOING WELL?

READ WHAT YOU WROTE ABOVE... WHAT DO YOU THINK YOU NEED TO #DoBetter ON PURPOSE TOMORROW?

MIND DUMP, PROCESS & UNRAVEL

If you have Accountability **YOU HAVE OWNERSHIP!**

MY DAILY NEWSLETTER
SELF REFLECTION = SELF AWARENESS

WHAT'S 1 THING IN THE *OUTSIDE* WORLD THAT AFFECTED ME TODAY?

WHAT ARE 1-2 THINGS I AM CONTENT WITH IN MY LIFE TODAY? THANKFUL? GRATEFUL?

WHAT 3 THINGS WENT ON TODAY IN *MY WORLD* THAT STOOD OUT? WHAT MADE AN IMPACT?

_____   _____   _____

WHAT DIDN'T GO WELL TODAY?

HOW DID I FEEL EMOTIONALLY? WRITE THEM OUT

HOW DID YOU FEEL PHYSICALLY? WHAT DO I NEED TO ADDRESS?
RESTRICTED BREATHING? ANXIOUSNESS? TENSION? GUT ISSUES? CHEST/BODY PAINS? WITHDRAWN?

ON THE OTHER HAND, WHAT DID GO WELL TODAY?

WHAT CONTRIBUTED TO THINGS GOING WELL?

READ WHAT YOU WROTE ABOVE...WHAT DO YOU THINK YOU NEED TO #DoBetter ON PURPOSE TOMORROW?

MIND DUMP, PROCESS & UNRAVEL

If you have Accountability **YOU HAVE OWNERSHIP!**

MY DAILY NEWSLETTER
SELF REFLECTION = SELF AWARENESS

WHAT'S 1 THING IN THE *OUTSIDE* WORLD THAT AFFECTED ME TODAY?

WHAT ARE 1-2 THINGS I AM CONTENT WITH IN MY LIFE TODAY? THANKFUL? GRATEFUL?

WHAT 3 THINGS WENT ON TODAY IN *MY WORLD* THAT STOOD OUT? WHAT MADE AN IMPACT?

WHAT DIDN'T GO WELL TODAY?

HOW DID I FEEL EMOTIONALLY? WRITE THEM OUT

HOW DID YOU FEEL PHYSICALLY? WHAT DO I NEED TO ADDRESS?
RESTRICTED BREATHING? ANXIOUSNESS? TENSION? GUT ISSUES? CHEST/BODY PAINS? WITHDRAWN?

ON THE OTHER HAND, WHAT DID GO WELL TODAY?

WHAT CONTRIBUTED TO THINGS GOING WELL?

READ WHAT YOU WROTE ABOVE...WHAT DO YOU THINK YOU NEED TO #DoBetter ON PURPOSE TOMORROW?

MIND DUMP, PROCESS & UNRAVEL

If you have Accountability **YOU HAVE OWNERSHIP!**

MY DAILY NEWSLETTER
SELF REFLECTION = SELF AWARENESS

WHAT'S 1 THING IN THE *OUTSIDE* WORLD THAT AFFECTED ME TODAY?

WHAT ARE 1-2 THINGS I AM CONTENT WITH IN MY LIFE TODAY? THANKFUL? GRATEFUL?

WHAT 3 THINGS WENT ON TODAY IN *MY WORLD* THAT STOOD OUT? WHAT MADE AN IMPACT?

_____   _____   _____

WHAT DIDN'T GO WELL TODAY?

HOW DID I FEEL EMOTIONALLY? WRITE THEM OUT

HOW DID YOU FEEL PHYSICALLY? WHAT DO I NEED TO ADDRESS?
RESTRICTED BREATHING? ANXIOUSNESS? TENSION? GUT ISSUES? CHEST/BODY PAINS? WITHDRAWN?

ON THE OTHER HAND, WHAT DID GO WELL TODAY?

WHAT CONTRIBUTED TO THINGS GOING WELL?

READ WHAT YOU WROTE ABOVE...WHAT DO YOU THINK YOU NEED TO #DoBetter ON PURPOSE TOMORROW?

MIND DUMP, PROCESS & UNRAVEL

If you have Accountability **YOU HAVE OWNERSHIP!**

MY DAILY NEWSLETTER
SELF REFLECTION = SELF AWARENESS

WHAT'S 1 THING IN THE *OUTSIDE* WORLD THAT AFFECTED ME TODAY?

WHAT ARE 1-2 THINGS I AM CONTENT WITH IN MY LIFE TODAY? THANKFUL? GRATEFUL?

WHAT 3 THINGS WENT ON TODAY IN *MY WORLD* THAT STOOD OUT? WHAT MADE AN IMPACT?

WHAT DIDN'T GO WELL TODAY?

HOW DID I FEEL EMOTIONALLY? WRITE THEM OUT

HOW DID YOU FEEL PHYSICALLY? WHAT DO I NEED TO ADDRESS?
RESTRICTED BREATHING? ANXIOUSNESS? TENSION? GUT ISSUES? CHEST/BODY PAINS? WITHDRAWN?

ON THE OTHER HAND, WHAT DID GO WELL TODAY?

WHAT CONTRIBUTED TO THINGS GOING WELL?

READ WHAT YOU WROTE ABOVE... WHAT DO YOU THINK YOU NEED TO #DOBETTER ON PURPOSE TOMORROW?

MIND DUMP, PROCESS & UNRAVEL

If you have Accountability **YOU HAVE OWNERSHIP!**

MY DAILY NEWSLETTER
SELF REFLECTION = SELF AWARENESS

What's 1 thing in the *OUTSIDE* world that Affected me today?

What are 1-2 things I am content with in my life today? Thankful? Grateful?

What 3 things went on today in *My world* that stood out? What made an impact?

What didn't go well today?

How did I feel emotionally? Write them out

How did you feel physically? What do I need to address? Restricted Breathing? Anxiousness? Tension? Gut issues? Chest/Body Pains? Withdrawn?

On the other hand, What did go well today?

What contributed to things going well?

Read what you wrote above...What do you think you need to #DoBetter on Purpose Tomorrow?

MIND DUMP, PROCESS & UNRAVEL

If you have Accountability **YOU HAVE OWNERSHIP!**

MY DAILY NEWSLETTER
SELF REFLECTION = SELF AWARENESS

WHAT'S 1 THING IN THE *OUTSIDE* WORLD THAT AFFECTED ME TODAY?

WHAT ARE 1-2 THINGS I AM CONTENT WITH IN MY LIFE TODAY? THANKFUL? GRATEFUL?

WHAT 3 THINGS WENT ON TODAY IN *MY WORLD* THAT STOOD OUT? WHAT MADE AN IMPACT?

WHAT DIDN'T GO WELL TODAY?

HOW DID I FEEL EMOTIONALLY? WRITE THEM OUT

HOW DID YOU FEEL PHYSICALLY? WHAT DO I NEED TO ADDRESS?
RESTRICTED BREATHING? ANXIOUSNESS? TENSION? GUT ISSUES? CHEST/BODY PAINS? WITHDRAWN?

ON THE OTHER HAND, WHAT DID GO WELL TODAY?

WHAT CONTRIBUTED TO THINGS GOING WELL?

READ WHAT YOU WROTE ABOVE…WHAT DO YOU THINK YOU NEED TO #DoBetter ON PURPOSE TOMORROW?

MIND DUMP, PROCESS & UNRAVEL

If you have Accountability **YOU HAVE OWNERSHIP!**

MY DAILY NEWSLETTER
SELF REFLECTION = SELF AWARENESS

WHAT'S 1 THING IN THE *OUTSIDE* WORLD THAT AFFECTED ME TODAY?

WHAT ARE 1-2 THINGS I AM CONTENT WITH IN MY LIFE TODAY? THANKFUL? GRATEFUL?

WHAT 3 THINGS WENT ON TODAY IN *MY WORLD* THAT STOOD OUT? WHAT MADE AN IMPACT?

_____   _____   _____

WHAT DIDN'T GO WELL TODAY?

HOW DID I FEEL EMOTIONALLY? WRITE THEM OUT

— ———————————— +

HOW DID YOU FEEL PHYSICALLY? WHAT DO I NEED TO ADDRESS?
RESTRICTED BREATHING? ANXIOUSNESS? TENSION? GUT ISSUES? CHEST/BODY PAINS? WITHDRAWN?

ON THE OTHER HAND, WHAT DID GO WELL TODAY?

WHAT CONTRIBUTED TO THINGS GOING WELL?

READ WHAT YOU WROTE ABOVE...WHAT DO YOU THINK YOU NEED TO #DoBetter ON PURPOSE TOMORROW?

MIND DUMP, PROCESS & UNRAVEL

If you have Accountability **YOU HAVE OWNERSHIP!**

MY DAILY NEWSLETTER
SELF REFLECTION = SELF AWARENESS

WHAT'S 1 THING IN THE *OUTSIDE* WORLD THAT AFFECTED ME TODAY?

WHAT ARE 1-2 THINGS I AM CONTENT WITH IN MY LIFE TODAY? THANKFUL? GRATEFUL?

WHAT 3 THINGS WENT ON TODAY IN *MY WORLD* THAT STOOD OUT? WHAT MADE AN IMPACT?

_____   _____   _____

WHAT DIDN'T GO WELL TODAY?

HOW DID I FEEL EMOTIONALLY? WRITE THEM OUT

HOW DID YOU FEEL PHYSICALLY? WHAT DO I NEED TO ADDRESS?
RESTRICTED BREATHING? ANXIOUSNESS? TENSION? GUT ISSUES? CHEST/BODY PAINS? WITHDRAWN?

ON THE OTHER HAND, WHAT DID GO WELL TODAY?

WHAT CONTRIBUTED TO THINGS GOING WELL?

READ WHAT YOU WROTE ABOVE... WHAT DO YOU THINK YOU NEED TO #DoBetter ON PURPOSE TOMORROW?

MIND DUMP, PROCESS & UNRAVEL

If you have Accountability **YOU HAVE OWNERSHIP!**

MY DAILY NEWSLETTER
SELF REFLECTION = SELF AWARENESS

WHAT'S 1 THING IN THE *OUTSIDE* WORLD THAT AFFECTED ME TODAY?

WHAT ARE 1-2 THINGS I AM CONTENT WITH IN MY LIFE TODAY? THANKFUL? GRATEFUL?

WHAT 3 THINGS WENT ON TODAY IN *MY WORLD* THAT STOOD OUT? WHAT MADE AN IMPACT?

WHAT DIDN'T GO WELL TODAY?

HOW DID I FEEL EMOTIONALLY? WRITE THEM OUT

HOW DID YOU FEEL PHYSICALLY? WHAT DO I NEED TO ADDRESS?
RESTRICTED BREATHING? ANXIOUSNESS? TENSION? GUT ISSUES? CHEST/BODY PAINS? WITHDRAWN?

ON THE OTHER HAND, WHAT DID GO WELL TODAY?

WHAT CONTRIBUTED TO THINGS GOING WELL?

READ WHAT YOU WROTE ABOVE...WHAT DO YOU THINK YOU NEED TO #DoBetter ON PURPOSE TOMORROW?

MIND DUMP, PROCESS & UNRAVEL

If you have Accountability **YOU HAVE OWNERSHIP!**

MY DAILY NEWSLETTER
SELF REFLECTION = SELF AWARENESS

WHAT'S 1 THING IN THE *OUTSIDE* WORLD THAT AFFECTED ME TODAY?

WHAT ARE 1-2 THINGS I AM CONTENT WITH IN MY LIFE TODAY? THANKFUL? GRATEFUL?

WHAT 3 THINGS WENT ON TODAY IN *MY WORLD* THAT STOOD OUT? WHAT MADE AN IMPACT?

WHAT DIDN'T GO WELL TODAY?

HOW DID I FEEL EMOTIONALLY? WRITE THEM OUT

HOW DID YOU FEEL PHYSICALLY? WHAT DO I NEED TO ADDRESS?
RESTRICTED BREATHING? ANXIOUSNESS? TENSION? GUT ISSUES? CHEST/BODY PAINS? WITHDRAWN?

ON THE OTHER HAND, WHAT DID GO WELL TODAY?

WHAT CONTRIBUTED TO THINGS GOING WELL?

READ WHAT YOU WROTE ABOVE…WHAT DO YOU THINK YOU NEED TO #DoBetter ON PURPOSE TOMORROW?

MIND DUMP, PROCESS & UNRAVEL

If you have Accountability **YOU HAVE OWNERSHIP!**

MY DAILY NEWSLETTER
SELF REFLECTION = SELF AWARENESS

WHAT'S 1 THING IN THE *OUTSIDE* WORLD THAT AFFECTED ME TODAY?

WHAT ARE 1-2 THINGS I AM CONTENT WITH IN MY LIFE TODAY? THANKFUL? GRATEFUL?

WHAT 3 THINGS WENT ON TODAY IN *MY WORLD* THAT STOOD OUT? WHAT MADE AN IMPACT?

_____   _____   _____

WHAT DIDN'T GO WELL TODAY?

HOW DID I FEEL EMOTIONALLY? WRITE THEM OUT

HOW DID YOU FEEL PHYSICALLY? WHAT DO I NEED TO ADDRESS?
RESTRICTED BREATHING? ANXIOUSNESS? TENSION? GUT ISSUES? CHEST/BODY PAINS? WITHDRAWN?

ON THE OTHER HAND, WHAT DID GO WELL TODAY?

WHAT CONTRIBUTED TO THINGS GOING WELL?

READ WHAT YOU WROTE ABOVE...WHAT DO YOU THINK YOU NEED TO #DoBetter ON PURPOSE TOMORROW?

MIND DUMP, PROCESS & UNRAVEL

If you have Accountability **YOU HAVE OWNERSHIP!**

MY DAILY NEWSLETTER
SELF REFLECTION = SELF AWARENESS

WHAT'S 1 THING IN THE *OUTSIDE* WORLD THAT AFFECTED ME TODAY?

WHAT ARE 1-2 THINGS I AM CONTENT WITH IN MY LIFE TODAY? THANKFUL? GRATEFUL?

WHAT 3 THINGS WENT ON TODAY IN *MY WORLD* THAT STOOD OUT? WHAT MADE AN IMPACT?

WHAT DIDN'T GO WELL TODAY?

HOW DID I FEEL EMOTIONALLY? WRITE THEM OUT

HOW DID YOU FEEL PHYSICALLY? WHAT DO I NEED TO ADDRESS?
RESTRICTED BREATHING? ANXIOUSNESS? TENSION? GUT ISSUES? CHEST/BODY PAINS? WITHDRAWN?

ON THE OTHER HAND, WHAT DID GO WELL TODAY?

WHAT CONTRIBUTED TO THINGS GOING WELL?

READ WHAT YOU WROTE ABOVE...WHAT DO YOU THINK YOU NEED TO #DoBetter ON PURPOSE TOMORROW?

MIND DUMP, PROCESS & UNRAVEL

If you have Accountability **YOU HAVE OWNERSHIP!**

MY DAILY NEWSLETTER
SELF REFLECTION = SELF AWARENESS

WHAT'S 1 THING IN THE *OUTSIDE* WORLD THAT AFFECTED ME TODAY?

WHAT ARE 1-2 THINGS I AM CONTENT WITH IN MY LIFE TODAY? THANKFUL? GRATEFUL?

WHAT 3 THINGS WENT ON TODAY IN *MY WORLD* THAT STOOD OUT? WHAT MADE AN IMPACT?

_____   _____   _____

WHAT DIDN'T GO WELL TODAY?

HOW DID I FEEL EMOTIONALLY? WRITE THEM OUT

☹ 🙁 😐 🙂 😊

— ▬▬▬▬▬▬▬▬▬▬ +

HOW DID YOU FEEL PHYSICALLY? WHAT DO I NEED TO ADDRESS?
RESTRICTED BREATHING? ANXIOUSNESS? TENSION? GUT ISSUES? CHEST/BODY PAINS? WITHDRAWN?

ON THE OTHER HAND, WHAT DID GO WELL TODAY?

WHAT CONTRIBUTED TO THINGS GOING WELL?

READ WHAT YOU WROTE ABOVE...WHAT DO YOU THINK YOU NEED TO #DOBETTER ON PURPOSE TOMORROW?

MIND DUMP, PROCESS & UNRAVEL

If you have Accountability **YOU HAVE OWNERSHIP!**

MY DAILY NEWSLETTER
SELF REFLECTION = SELF AWARENESS

WHAT'S 1 THING IN THE *OUTSIDE* WORLD THAT AFFECTED ME TODAY?

WHAT ARE 1-2 THINGS I AM CONTENT WITH IN MY LIFE TODAY? THANKFUL? GRATEFUL?

WHAT 3 THINGS WENT ON TODAY IN *MY WORLD* THAT STOOD OUT? WHAT MADE AN IMPACT?

_____   _____   _____

WHAT DIDN'T GO WELL TODAY?

HOW DID I FEEL EMOTIONALLY? WRITE THEM OUT

☹ 🙁 😐 🙂 😊

− ▬▬▬▬▬▬▬▬▬▬ +

HOW DID YOU FEEL PHYSICALLY? WHAT DO I NEED TO ADDRESS?
RESTRICTED BREATHING? ANXIOUSNESS? TENSION? GUT ISSUES? CHEST/BODY PAINS? WITHDRAWN?

ON THE OTHER HAND, WHAT DID GO WELL TODAY?

WHAT CONTRIBUTED TO THINGS GOING WELL?

READ WHAT YOU WROTE ABOVE… WHAT DO YOU THINK YOU NEED TO #DoBetter ON PURPOSE TOMORROW?

MIND DUMP, PROCESS & UNRAVEL

If you have Accountability **YOU HAVE OWNERSHIP!**

MY DAILY NEWSLETTER
SELF REFLECTION = SELF AWARENESS

WHAT'S 1 THING IN THE *OUTSIDE* WORLD THAT AFFECTED ME TODAY?

WHAT ARE 1-2 THINGS I AM CONTENT WITH IN MY LIFE TODAY? THANKFUL? GRATEFUL?

WHAT 3 THINGS WENT ON TODAY IN *MY WORLD* THAT STOOD OUT? WHAT MADE AN IMPACT?

_____   _____   _____

WHAT DIDN'T GO WELL TODAY?

_____
_____
_____
_____
_____

HOW DID I FEEL EMOTIONALLY? WRITE THEM OUT

— _____ +

_____
_____
_____
_____

HOW DID YOU FEEL PHYSICALLY? WHAT DO I NEED TO ADDRESS?
RESTRICTED BREATHING? ANXIOUSNESS? TENSION? GUT ISSUES? CHEST/BODY PAINS? WITHDRAWN?

_____

ON THE OTHER HAND, WHAT DID GO WELL TODAY?

_____
_____
_____
_____
_____

WHAT CONTRIBUTED TO THINGS GOING WELL?

_____
_____
_____
_____
_____

READ WHAT YOU WROTE ABOVE…WHAT DO YOU THINK YOU NEED TO #DoBetter ON PURPOSE TOMORROW?

_____
_____

MIND DUMP, PROCESS & UNRAVEL

If you have Accountability **YOU HAVE OWNERSHIP!**

MY DAILY NEWSLETTER
SELF REFLECTION = SELF AWARENESS

WHAT'S 1 THING IN THE *OUTSIDE* WORLD THAT AFFECTED ME TODAY?

WHAT ARE 1-2 THINGS I AM CONTENT WITH IN MY LIFE TODAY? THANKFUL? GRATEFUL?

WHAT 3 THINGS WENT ON TODAY IN *MY WORLD* THAT STOOD OUT? WHAT MADE AN IMPACT?

WHAT DIDN'T GO WELL TODAY?

HOW DID I FEEL EMOTIONALLY? WRITE THEM OUT

HOW DID YOU FEEL PHYSICALLY? WHAT DO I NEED TO ADDRESS?
RESTRICTED BREATHING? ANXIOUSNESS? TENSION? GUT ISSUES? CHEST/BODY PAINS? WITHDRAWN?

ON THE OTHER HAND, WHAT DID GO WELL TODAY?

WHAT CONTRIBUTED TO THINGS GOING WELL?

READ WHAT YOU WROTE ABOVE...WHAT DO YOU THINK YOU NEED TO #DoBetter ON PURPOSE TOMORROW?

MIND DUMP, PROCESS & UNRAVEL

If you have Accountability **YOU HAVE OWNERSHIP!**

MY DAILY NEWSLETTER
SELF REFLECTION = SELF AWARENESS

WHAT'S 1 THING IN THE *OUTSIDE* WORLD THAT AFFECTED ME TODAY?

WHAT ARE 1-2 THINGS I AM CONTENT WITH IN MY LIFE TODAY? THANKFUL? GRATEFUL?

WHAT 3 THINGS WENT ON TODAY IN *MY WORLD* THAT STOOD OUT? WHAT MADE AN IMPACT?

WHAT DIDN'T GO WELL TODAY?

HOW DID I FEEL EMOTIONALLY? WRITE THEM OUT

HOW DID YOU FEEL PHYSICALLY? WHAT DO I NEED TO ADDRESS? RESTRICTED BREATHING? ANXIOUSNESS? TENSION? GUT ISSUES? CHEST/BODY PAINS? WITHDRAWN?

ON THE OTHER HAND, WHAT DID GO WELL TODAY?

WHAT CONTRIBUTED TO THINGS GOING WELL?

READ WHAT YOU WROTE ABOVE...WHAT DO YOU THINK YOU NEED TO #DoBetter ON PURPOSE TOMORROW?

MIND DUMP, PROCESS & UNRAVEL

If you have Accountability **YOU HAVE OWNERSHIP!**

MY DAILY NEWSLETTER
SELF REFLECTION = SELF AWARENESS

WHAT'S 1 THING IN THE *OUTSIDE* WORLD THAT AFFECTED ME TODAY?

WHAT ARE 1-2 THINGS I AM CONTENT WITH IN MY LIFE TODAY? THANKFUL? GRATEFUL?

WHAT 3 THINGS WENT ON TODAY IN *MY WORLD* THAT STOOD OUT? WHAT MADE AN IMPACT?

WHAT DIDN'T GO WELL TODAY?

HOW DID I FEEL EMOTIONALLY? WRITE THEM OUT

HOW DID YOU FEEL PHYSICALLY? WHAT DO I NEED TO ADDRESS?
RESTRICTED BREATHING? ANXIOUSNESS? TENSION? GUT ISSUES? CHEST/BODY PAINS? WITHDRAWN?

ON THE OTHER HAND, WHAT DID GO WELL TODAY?

WHAT CONTRIBUTED TO THINGS GOING WELL?

READ WHAT YOU WROTE ABOVE... WHAT DO YOU THINK YOU NEED TO #DoBetter ON PURPOSE TOMORROW?

MIND DUMP, PROCESS & UNRAVEL

If you have Accountability **YOU HAVE OWNERSHIP!**

MY DAILY NEWSLETTER
SELF REFLECTION = SELF AWARENESS

WHAT'S 1 THING IN THE *OUTSIDE* WORLD THAT AFFECTED ME TODAY?

WHAT ARE 1-2 THINGS I AM CONTENT WITH IN MY LIFE TODAY? THANKFUL? GRATEFUL?

WHAT 3 THINGS WENT ON TODAY IN *MY WORLD* THAT STOOD OUT? WHAT MADE AN IMPACT?

WHAT DIDN'T GO WELL TODAY?

HOW DID I FEEL EMOTIONALLY? WRITE THEM OUT

HOW DID YOU FEEL PHYSICALLY? WHAT DO I NEED TO ADDRESS?
RESTRICTED BREATHING? ANXIOUSNESS? TENSION? GUT ISSUES? CHEST/BODY PAINS? WITHDRAWN?

ON THE OTHER HAND, WHAT DID GO WELL TODAY?

WHAT CONTRIBUTED TO THINGS GOING WELL?

READ WHAT YOU WROTE ABOVE…WHAT DO YOU THINK YOU NEED TO #DoBetter ON PURPOSE TOMORROW?

MIND DUMP, PROCESS & UNRAVEL

If you have Accountability **YOU HAVE OWNERSHIP!**

MY DAILY NEWSLETTER
SELF REFLECTION = SELF AWARENESS

WHAT'S 1 THING IN THE *OUTSIDE* WORLD THAT AFFECTED ME TODAY?

WHAT ARE 1-2 THINGS I AM CONTENT WITH IN MY LIFE TODAY? THANKFUL? GRATEFUL?

WHAT 3 THINGS WENT ON TODAY IN *MY WORLD* THAT STOOD OUT? WHAT MADE AN IMPACT?

_____   _____   _____

WHAT DIDN'T GO WELL TODAY?

HOW DID I FEEL EMOTIONALLY? WRITE THEM OUT

☹ 🙁 😐 🙂 😊

− ▬▬▬▬▬▬▬▬▬▬ +

HOW DID YOU FEEL PHYSICALLY? WHAT DO I NEED TO ADDRESS?
RESTRICTED BREATHING? ANXIOUSNESS? TENSION? GUT ISSUES? CHEST/BODY PAINS? WITHDRAWN?

ON THE OTHER HAND, WHAT DID GO WELL TODAY?

WHAT CONTRIBUTED TO THINGS GOING WELL?

READ WHAT YOU WROTE ABOVE...WHAT DO YOU THINK YOU NEED TO #DoBetter ON PURPOSE TOMORROW?

MIND DUMP, PROCESS & UNRAVEL

If you have Accountability YOU HAVE OWNERSHIP!

MY DAILY NEWSLETTER
SELF REFLECTION = SELF AWARENESS

WHAT'S 1 THING IN THE *OUTSIDE* WORLD THAT AFFECTED ME TODAY?

WHAT ARE 1-2 THINGS I AM CONTENT WITH IN MY LIFE TODAY? THANKFUL? GRATEFUL?

WHAT 3 THINGS WENT ON TODAY IN *MY WORLD* THAT STOOD OUT? WHAT MADE AN IMPACT?

WHAT DIDN'T GO WELL TODAY?

HOW DID I FEEL EMOTIONALLY? WRITE THEM OUT

HOW DID YOU FEEL PHYSICALLY? WHAT DO I NEED TO ADDRESS?
RESTRICTED BREATHING? ANXIOUSNESS? TENSION? GUT ISSUES? CHEST/BODY PAINS? WITHDRAWN?

ON THE OTHER HAND, WHAT DID GO WELL TODAY?

WHAT CONTRIBUTED TO THINGS GOING WELL?

READ WHAT YOU WROTE ABOVE… WHAT DO YOU THINK YOU NEED TO #DoBetter ON PURPOSE TOMORROW?

MIND DUMP, PROCESS & UNRAVEL

If you have Accountability **YOU HAVE OWNERSHIP!**

MY DAILY NEWSLETTER
SELF REFLECTION = SELF AWARENESS

WHAT'S 1 THING IN THE *OUTSIDE* WORLD THAT AFFECTED ME TODAY?

WHAT ARE 1-2 THINGS I AM CONTENT WITH IN MY LIFE TODAY? THANKFUL? GRATEFUL?

WHAT 3 THINGS WENT ON TODAY IN *MY WORLD* THAT STOOD OUT? WHAT MADE AN IMPACT?

_____   _____   _____

WHAT DIDN'T GO WELL TODAY?

_____
_____
_____
_____

HOW DID I FEEL EMOTIONALLY? WRITE THEM OUT

☹ 🙁 😐 🙂 😊

− ▬▬▬▬▬▬▬▬▬▬ +

_____
_____
_____
_____

HOW DID YOU FEEL PHYSICALLY? WHAT DO I NEED TO ADDRESS?
RESTRICTED BREATHING? ANXIOUSNESS? TENSION? GUT ISSUES? CHEST/BODY PAINS? WITHDRAWN?

_____

ON THE OTHER HAND, WHAT DID GO WELL TODAY?

_____
_____
_____
_____
_____

WHAT CONTRIBUTED TO THINGS GOING WELL?

_____
_____
_____
_____
_____

READ WHAT YOU WROTE ABOVE…WHAT DO YOU THINK YOU NEED TO #DoBetter ON PURPOSE TOMORROW?

_____
_____

MIND DUMP, PROCESS & UNRAVEL

If you have Accountability **YOU HAVE OWNERSHIP!**

MY DAILY NEWSLETTER
SELF REFLECTION = SELF AWARENESS

WHAT'S 1 THING IN THE *OUTSIDE* WORLD THAT AFFECTED ME TODAY?

WHAT ARE 1-2 THINGS I AM CONTENT WITH IN MY LIFE TODAY? THANKFUL? GRATEFUL?

WHAT 3 THINGS WENT ON TODAY IN *MY WORLD* THAT STOOD OUT? WHAT MADE AN IMPACT?

_____   _____   _____

WHAT DIDN'T GO WELL TODAY?

HOW DID I FEEL EMOTIONALLY? WRITE THEM OUT

HOW DID YOU FEEL PHYSICALLY? WHAT DO I NEED TO ADDRESS?
RESTRICTED BREATHING? ANXIOUSNESS? TENSION? GUT ISSUES? CHEST/BODY PAINS? WITHDRAWN?

ON THE OTHER HAND, WHAT DID GO WELL TODAY?

WHAT CONTRIBUTED TO THINGS GOING WELL?

READ WHAT YOU WROTE ABOVE...WHAT DO YOU THINK YOU NEED TO #DoBetter ON PURPOSE TOMORROW?

MIND DUMP, PROCESS & UNRAVEL

If you have Accountability **YOU HAVE OWNERSHIP!**

MY DAILY NEWSLETTER
SELF REFLECTION = SELF AWARENESS

WHAT'S 1 THING IN THE *OUTSIDE* WORLD THAT AFFECTED ME TODAY?

WHAT ARE 1-2 THINGS I AM CONTENT WITH IN MY LIFE TODAY? THANKFUL? GRATEFUL?

WHAT 3 THINGS WENT ON TODAY IN *MY WORLD* THAT STOOD OUT? WHAT MADE AN IMPACT?

WHAT DIDN'T GO WELL TODAY?

HOW DID I FEEL EMOTIONALLY? WRITE THEM OUT

HOW DID YOU FEEL PHYSICALLY? WHAT DO I NEED TO ADDRESS?
RESTRICTED BREATHING? ANXIOUSNESS? TENSION? GUT ISSUES? CHEST/BODY PAINS? WITHDRAWN?

ON THE OTHER HAND, WHAT DID GO WELL TODAY?

WHAT CONTRIBUTED TO THINGS GOING WELL?

READ WHAT YOU WROTE ABOVE... WHAT DO YOU THINK YOU NEED TO #DoBetter ON PURPOSE TOMORROW?

MIND DUMP, PROCESS & UNRAVEL

If you have Accountability **YOU HAVE OWNERSHIP!**

MY DAILY NEWSLETTER
SELF REFLECTION = SELF AWARENESS

WHAT'S 1 THING IN THE *OUTSIDE* WORLD THAT AFFECTED ME TODAY?

WHAT ARE 1-2 THINGS I AM CONTENT WITH IN MY LIFE TODAY? THANKFUL? GRATEFUL?

WHAT 3 THINGS WENT ON TODAY IN *MY WORLD* THAT STOOD OUT? WHAT MADE AN IMPACT?

WHAT DIDN'T GO WELL TODAY?

HOW DID I FEEL EMOTIONALLY? WRITE THEM OUT

HOW DID YOU FEEL PHYSICALLY? WHAT DO I NEED TO ADDRESS?
RESTRICTED BREATHING? ANXIOUSNESS? TENSION? GUT ISSUES? CHEST/BODY PAINS? WITHDRAWN?

ON THE OTHER HAND, WHAT DID GO WELL TODAY?

WHAT CONTRIBUTED TO THINGS GOING WELL?

READ WHAT YOU WROTE ABOVE...WHAT DO YOU THINK YOU NEED TO #DoBetter ON PURPOSE TOMORROW?

MIND DUMP, PROCESS & UNRAVEL

If you take Responsibility
YOU HAVE OWNERSHIP!
ANSWER THESE QUESTIONS BELOW TO DEFINE YOUR PLAN FORWARD NEXT MONTH

WHERE DO YOU NEED TO DRAW A LINE TO #DOBETTER ON PURPOSE?

_____

_____

_____

_____

_____

WHAT HABIT DO YOU NEED TO WORK ON TO #DOBETTER ON PURPOSE?

_____

_____

WHAT'S 1 EMOTION I WILL I FOCUS ON TO GET UNDER CONTROL?

WHAT WILL MOTIVATE YOU TO #DOBETTER ON PURPOSE?

_____

_____

_____

_____

_____

WHAT NEEDS TO BE UNRAVELED ABOUT THIS PAST MONTH?

_____

_____

_____

_____

_____

MIND DUMP, PROCESS & UNRAVEL

Self Awareness Alignment

Outline in these categories where you will *FOCUS* your self reflection
What things will you keep in the front of your mind?

RELATIONSHIPS

HEALTH

FINANCES

LESIURE

CAREER

SPIRITUALITY

GROWTH

NOTES:
_____
_____

Intentional Habits
HOW WILL YOU BE INTENTIONAL?

REMEBER THESE IN YOUR DAILY REFLECTIONS

MORNING HABITS   *MID-DAY HABITS*   *EVENING HABITS*

WHAT **DISCIPLINES** WILL YOU PUT INTO PLACE?

WHAT WILL BE YOUR **WINNING STRATEGI**ES TO CHANGE WHAT YOU SEE ON A DAILY BASIS?

TRY: PRAYER/MEDITATION, WRITTEN REMINDERS, AND ACCOUNTABILITY PARTNERS...

WRITE BELOW 2-3 THINGS YOU ARE WILLING TO COMMIT TO DOING TO CHANGE BEHAVIORS (THINK IT, SPEAK IT, WRITE IT, WORK IT)

▶

▶

▶

If you have Accountability **YOU HAVE OWNERSHIP!**

MY DAILY NEWSLETTER
SELF REFLECTION = SELF AWARENESS

WHAT'S 1 THING IN THE *OUTSIDE* WORLD THAT AFFECTED ME TODAY?

WHAT ARE 1-2 THINGS I AM CONTENT WITH IN MY LIFE TODAY? THANKFUL? GRATEFUL?

WHAT 3 THINGS WENT ON TODAY IN *MY WORLD* THAT STOOD OUT? WHAT MADE AN IMPACT?

WHAT DIDN'T GO WELL TODAY?

HOW DID I FEEL EMOTIONALLY? WRITE THEM OUT

HOW DID YOU FEEL PHYSICALLY? WHAT DO I NEED TO ADDRESS?
RESTRICTED BREATHING? ANXIOUSNESS? TENSION? GUT ISSUES? CHEST/BODY PAINS? WITHDRAWN?

ON THE OTHER HAND, WHAT DID GO WELL TODAY?

WHAT CONTRIBUTED TO THINGS GOING WELL?

READ WHAT YOU WROTE ABOVE...WHAT DO YOU THINK YOU NEED TO #DoBetter ON PURPOSE TOMORROW?

MIND DUMP, PROCESS & UNRAVEL

If you have Accountability **YOU HAVE OWNERSHIP!**

MY DAILY NEWSLETTER
SELF REFLECTION = SELF AWARENESS

WHAT'S 1 THING IN THE *OUTSIDE* WORLD THAT AFFECTED ME TODAY?

WHAT ARE 1-2 THINGS I AM CONTENT WITH IN MY LIFE TODAY? THANKFUL? GRATEFUL?

WHAT 3 THINGS WENT ON TODAY IN *MY WORLD* THAT STOOD OUT? WHAT MADE AN IMPACT?

_____   _____   _____

WHAT DIDN'T GO WELL TODAY?

HOW DID I FEEL EMOTIONALLY? WRITE THEM OUT

− _____ +

HOW DID YOU FEEL PHYSICALLY? WHAT DO I NEED TO ADDRESS?
RESTRICTED BREATHING? ANXIOUSNESS? TENSION? GUT ISSUES? CHEST/BODY PAINS? WITHDRAWN?

ON THE OTHER HAND, WHAT DID GO WELL TODAY?

WHAT CONTRIBUTED TO THINGS GOING WELL?

READ WHAT YOU WROTE ABOVE...WHAT DO YOU THINK YOU NEED TO #DoBetter ON PURPOSE TOMORROW?

MIND DUMP, PROCESS & UNRAVEL

If you have Accountability **YOU HAVE OWNERSHIP!**

MY DAILY NEWSLETTER
SELF REFLECTION = SELF AWARENESS

WHAT'S 1 THING IN THE *OUTSIDE* WORLD THAT AFFECTED ME TODAY?

WHAT ARE 1-2 THINGS I AM CONTENT WITH IN MY LIFE TODAY? THANKFUL? GRATEFUL?

WHAT 3 THINGS WENT ON TODAY IN *MY WORLD* THAT STOOD OUT? WHAT MADE AN IMPACT?

_____ _____ _____

WHAT DIDN'T GO WELL TODAY?

_____
_____
_____
_____

HOW DID I FEEL EMOTIONALLY? WRITE THEM OUT

☹ 🙁 😐 🙂 😊
– ═══════════ +

_____
_____
_____
_____

HOW DID YOU FEEL PHYSICALLY? WHAT DO I NEED TO ADDRESS?
RESTRICTED BREATHING? ANXIOUSNESS? TENSION? GUT ISSUES? CHEST/BODY PAINS? WITHDRAWN?

_____

ON THE OTHER HAND, WHAT DID GO WELL TODAY?

_____
_____
_____
_____
_____

WHAT CONTRIBUTED TO THINGS GOING WELL?

_____
_____
_____
_____
_____

READ WHAT YOU WROTE ABOVE... WHAT DO YOU THINK YOU NEED TO #DoBetter ON PURPOSE TOMORROW?

_____
_____

MIND DUMP, PROCESS & UNRAVEL

If you have Accountability **YOU HAVE OWNERSHIP!**

MY DAILY NEWSLETTER
SELF REFLECTION = SELF AWARENESS

WHAT'S 1 THING IN THE *OUTSIDE* WORLD THAT AFFECTED ME TODAY?
_____

WHAT ARE 1-2 THINGS I AM CONTENT WITH IN MY LIFE TODAY? THANKFUL? GRATEFUL?

WHAT 3 THINGS WENT ON TODAY IN *MY WORLD* THAT STOOD OUT? WHAT MADE AN IMPACT?
_____   _____   _____

WHAT DIDN'T GO WELL TODAY?
_____
_____
_____
_____

HOW DID I FEEL EMOTIONALLY? WRITE THEM OUT
☹ 🙁 😐 🙂 😊
− ▬▬▬▬▬▬▬▬▬▬ +
_____
_____
_____

HOW DID YOU FEEL PHYSICALLY? WHAT DO I NEED TO ADDRESS?
RESTRICTED BREATHING? ANXIOUSNESS? TENSION? GUT ISSUES? CHEST/BODY PAINS? WITHDRAWN?
_____

ON THE OTHER HAND, WHAT DID GO WELL TODAY?
_____
_____
_____
_____
_____

WHAT CONTRIBUTED TO THINGS GOING WELL?
_____
_____
_____
_____
_____

READ WHAT YOU WROTE ABOVE...WHAT DO YOU THINK YOU NEED TO #DOBETTER ON PURPOSE TOMORROW?
_____
_____

MIND DUMP, PROCESS & UNRAVEL

If you have Accountability **YOU HAVE OWNERSHIP!**

MY DAILY NEWSLETTER
SELF REFLECTION = SELF AWARENESS

WHAT'S 1 THING IN THE *OUTSIDE* WORLD THAT AFFECTED ME TODAY?

WHAT ARE 1-2 THINGS I AM CONTENT WITH IN MY LIFE TODAY? THANKFUL? GRATEFUL?

WHAT 3 THINGS WENT ON TODAY IN *MY WORLD* THAT STOOD OUT? WHAT MADE AN IMPACT?

_____   _____   _____

WHAT DIDN'T GO WELL TODAY?

HOW DID I FEEL EMOTIONALLY? WRITE THEM OUT

— _____ +

HOW DID YOU FEEL PHYSICALLY? WHAT DO I NEED TO ADDRESS?
RESTRICTED BREATHING? ANXIOUSNESS? TENSION? GUT ISSUES? CHEST/BODY PAINS? WITHDRAWN?

ON THE OTHER HAND, WHAT DID GO WELL TODAY?

WHAT CONTRIBUTED TO THINGS GOING WELL?

READ WHAT YOU WROTE ABOVE… WHAT DO YOU THINK YOU NEED TO #DoBetter ON PURPOSE TOMORROW?

MIND DUMP, PROCESS & UNRAVEL

If you have Accountability **YOU HAVE OWNERSHIP!**

MY DAILY NEWSLETTER
SELF REFLECTION = SELF AWARENESS

WHAT'S 1 THING IN THE *OUTSIDE* WORLD THAT AFFECTED ME TODAY?

WHAT ARE 1-2 THINGS I AM CONTENT WITH IN MY LIFE TODAY? THANKFUL? GRATEFUL?

WHAT 3 THINGS WENT ON TODAY IN *MY WORLD* THAT STOOD OUT? WHAT MADE AN IMPACT?

WHAT DIDN'T GO WELL TODAY?

HOW DID I FEEL EMOTIONALLY? WRITE THEM OUT

HOW DID YOU FEEL PHYSICALLY? WHAT DO I NEED TO ADDRESS?
RESTRICTED BREATHING? ANXIOUSNESS? TENSION? GUT ISSUES? CHEST/BODY PAINS? WITHDRAWN?

ON THE OTHER HAND, WHAT DID GO WELL TODAY?

WHAT CONTRIBUTED TO THINGS GOING WELL?

READ WHAT YOU WROTE ABOVE...WHAT DO YOU THINK YOU NEED TO #DoBetter ON PURPOSE TOMORROW?

MIND DUMP, PROCESS & UNRAVEL

If you have Accountability **YOU HAVE OWNERSHIP!**

MY DAILY NEWSLETTER
SELF REFLECTION = SELF AWARENESS

WHAT'S 1 THING IN THE *OUTSIDE* WORLD THAT AFFECTED ME TODAY?

WHAT ARE 1-2 THINGS I AM CONTENT WITH IN MY LIFE TODAY? THANKFUL? GRATEFUL?

WHAT 3 THINGS WENT ON TODAY IN *MY WORLD* THAT STOOD OUT? WHAT MADE AN IMPACT?

WHAT DIDN'T GO WELL TODAY?

HOW DID I FEEL EMOTIONALLY? WRITE THEM OUT

HOW DID YOU FEEL PHYSICALLY? WHAT DO I NEED TO ADDRESS?
RESTRICTED BREATHING? ANXIOUSNESS? TENSION? GUT ISSUES? CHEST/BODY PAINS? WITHDRAWN?

ON THE OTHER HAND, WHAT DID GO WELL TODAY?

WHAT CONTRIBUTED TO THINGS GOING WELL?

READ WHAT YOU WROTE ABOVE…WHAT DO YOU THINK YOU NEED TO #DoBetter ON PURPOSE TOMORROW?

MIND DUMP, PROCESS & UNRAVEL

If you have Accountability **YOU HAVE OWNERSHIP!**

MY DAILY NEWSLETTER
SELF REFLECTION = SELF AWARENESS

WHAT'S 1 THING IN THE *OUTSIDE* WORLD THAT AFFECTED ME TODAY?

WHAT ARE 1-2 THINGS I AM CONTENT WITH IN MY LIFE TODAY? THANKFUL? GRATEFUL?

WHAT 3 THINGS WENT ON TODAY IN *MY WORLD* THAT STOOD OUT? WHAT MADE AN IMPACT?

_____   _____   _____

WHAT DIDN'T GO WELL TODAY?

_____
_____
_____
_____

HOW DID I FEEL EMOTIONALLY? WRITE THEM OUT

– ▬▬▬▬▬▬▬▬▬▬ +

_____
_____
_____

HOW DID YOU FEEL PHYSICALLY? WHAT DO I NEED TO ADDRESS?
RESTRICTED BREATHING? ANXIOUSNESS? TENSION? GUT ISSUES? CHEST/BODY PAINS? WITHDRAWN?

_____

ON THE OTHER HAND, WHAT DID GO WELL TODAY?

_____
_____
_____
_____
_____

WHAT CONTRIBUTED TO THINGS GOING WELL?

_____
_____
_____
_____
_____

READ WHAT YOU WROTE ABOVE…WHAT DO YOU THINK YOU NEED TO #DoBetter ON PURPOSE TOMORROW?

_____
_____

MIND DUMP, PROCESS & UNRAVEL

If you have Accountability **YOU HAVE OWNERSHIP!**

MY DAILY NEWSLETTER
SELF REFLECTION = SELF AWARENESS

WHAT'S 1 THING IN THE *OUTSIDE* WORLD THAT AFFECTED ME TODAY?

WHAT ARE 1-2 THINGS I AM CONTENT WITH IN MY LIFE TODAY? THANKFUL? GRATEFUL?

WHAT 3 THINGS WENT ON TODAY IN *MY WORLD* THAT STOOD OUT? WHAT MADE AN IMPACT?

WHAT DIDN'T GO WELL TODAY?

HOW DID I FEEL EMOTIONALLY? WRITE THEM OUT

HOW DID YOU FEEL PHYSICALLY? WHAT DO I NEED TO ADDRESS?
RESTRICTED BREATHING? ANXIOUSNESS? TENSION? GUT ISSUES? CHEST/BODY PAINS? WITHDRAWN?

ON THE OTHER HAND, WHAT DID GO WELL TODAY?

WHAT CONTRIBUTED TO THINGS GOING WELL?

READ WHAT YOU WROTE ABOVE... WHAT DO YOU THINK YOU NEED TO #DoBetter ON PURPOSE TOMORROW?

MIND DUMP, PROCESS & UNRAVEL

If you have Accountability **YOU HAVE OWNERSHIP!**

MY DAILY NEWSLETTER
SELF REFLECTION = SELF AWARENESS

WHAT'S 1 THING IN THE *OUTSIDE* WORLD THAT AFFECTED ME TODAY?

WHAT ARE 1-2 THINGS I AM CONTENT WITH IN MY LIFE TODAY? THANKFUL? GRATEFUL?

WHAT 3 THINGS WENT ON TODAY IN *MY WORLD* THAT STOOD OUT? WHAT MADE AN IMPACT?

WHAT DIDN'T GO WELL TODAY?

HOW DID I FEEL EMOTIONALLY? WRITE THEM OUT

HOW DID YOU FEEL PHYSICALLY? WHAT DO I NEED TO ADDRESS?
RESTRICTED BREATHING? ANXIOUSNESS? TENSION? GUT ISSUES? CHEST/BODY PAINS? WITHDRAWN?

ON THE OTHER HAND, WHAT DID GO WELL TODAY?

WHAT CONTRIBUTED TO THINGS GOING WELL?

READ WHAT YOU WROTE ABOVE... WHAT DO YOU THINK YOU NEED TO #DoBetter ON PURPOSE TOMORROW?

MIND DUMP, PROCESS & UNRAVEL

If you have Accountability **YOU HAVE OWNERSHIP!**

MY DAILY NEWSLETTER
SELF REFLECTION = SELF AWARENESS

WHAT'S 1 THING IN THE *OUTSIDE* WORLD THAT AFFECTED ME TODAY?

WHAT ARE 1-2 THINGS I AM CONTENT WITH IN MY LIFE TODAY? THANKFUL? GRATEFUL?

WHAT 3 THINGS WENT ON TODAY IN *MY WORLD* THAT STOOD OUT? WHAT MADE AN IMPACT?

_____   _____   _____

WHAT DIDN'T GO WELL TODAY?

HOW DID I FEEL EMOTIONALLY? WRITE THEM OUT

😟 😕 😐 🙂 😊
− ▬▬▬▬▬▬▬▬▬ +

HOW DID YOU FEEL PHYSICALLY? WHAT DO I NEED TO ADDRESS?
RESTRICTED BREATHING? ANXIOUSNESS? TENSION? GUT ISSUES? CHEST/BODY PAINS? WITHDRAWN?

ON THE OTHER HAND, WHAT DID GO WELL TODAY?

WHAT CONTRIBUTED TO THINGS GOING WELL?

READ WHAT YOU WROTE ABOVE…WHAT DO YOU THINK YOU NEED TO #DoBetter ON PURPOSE TOMORROW?

MIND DUMP, PROCESS & UNRAVEL

If you have Accountability **YOU HAVE OWNERSHIP!**

MY DAILY NEWSLETTER
SELF REFLECTION = SELF AWARENESS

WHAT'S 1 THING IN THE *OUTSIDE* WORLD THAT AFFECTED ME TODAY?

WHAT ARE 1-2 THINGS I AM CONTENT WITH IN MY LIFE TODAY? THANKFUL? GRATEFUL?

WHAT 3 THINGS WENT ON TODAY IN *MY WORLD* THAT STOOD OUT? WHAT MADE AN IMPACT?

_____   _____   _____

WHAT DIDN'T GO WELL TODAY?

HOW DID I FEEL EMOTIONALLY? WRITE THEM OUT

— ▬▬▬▬▬▬▬▬▬▬ +

HOW DID YOU FEEL PHYSICALLY? WHAT DO I NEED TO ADDRESS?
RESTRICTED BREATHING? ANXIOUSNESS? TENSION? GUT ISSUES? CHEST/BODY PAINS? WITHDRAWN?

ON THE OTHER HAND, WHAT DID GO WELL TODAY?

WHAT CONTRIBUTED TO THINGS GOING WELL?

READ WHAT YOU WROTE ABOVE...WHAT DO YOU THINK YOU NEED TO #DoBetter ON PURPOSE TOMORROW?

MIND DUMP, PROCESS & UNRAVEL

If you have Accountability **YOU HAVE OWNERSHIP!**

MY DAILY NEWSLETTER
SELF REFLECTION = SELF AWARENESS

WHAT'S 1 THING IN THE *OUTSIDE* WORLD THAT AFFECTED ME TODAY?

WHAT ARE 1-2 THINGS I AM CONTENT WITH IN MY LIFE TODAY? THANKFUL? GRATEFUL?

WHAT 3 THINGS WENT ON TODAY IN *MY WORLD* THAT STOOD OUT? WHAT MADE AN IMPACT?

WHAT DIDN'T GO WELL TODAY?

HOW DID I FEEL EMOTIONALLY? WRITE THEM OUT

HOW DID YOU FEEL PHYSICALLY? WHAT DO I NEED TO ADDRESS?
RESTRICTED BREATHING? ANXIOUSNESS? TENSION? GUT ISSUES? CHEST/BODY PAINS? WITHDRAWN?

ON THE OTHER HAND, WHAT DID GO WELL TODAY?

WHAT CONTRIBUTED TO THINGS GOING WELL?

READ WHAT YOU WROTE ABOVE... WHAT DO YOU THINK YOU NEED TO #DoBetter ON PURPOSE TOMORROW?

MIND DUMP, PROCESS & UNRAVEL

If you have Accountability **YOU HAVE OWNERSHIP!**

MY DAILY NEWSLETTER
SELF REFLECTION = SELF AWARENESS

WHAT'S 1 THING IN THE *OUTSIDE* WORLD THAT AFFECTED ME TODAY?

WHAT ARE 1-2 THINGS I AM CONTENT WITH IN MY LIFE TODAY? THANKFUL? GRATEFUL?

WHAT 3 THINGS WENT ON TODAY IN *MY WORLD* THAT STOOD OUT? WHAT MADE AN IMPACT?

_____   _____   _____

WHAT DIDN'T GO WELL TODAY?

HOW DID I FEEL EMOTIONALLY? WRITE THEM OUT

HOW DID YOU FEEL PHYSICALLY? WHAT DO I NEED TO ADDRESS?
RESTRICTED BREATHING? ANXIOUSNESS? TENSION? GUT ISSUES? CHEST/BODY PAINS? WITHDRAWN?

ON THE OTHER HAND, WHAT DID GO WELL TODAY?

WHAT CONTRIBUTED TO THINGS GOING WELL?

READ WHAT YOU WROTE ABOVE...WHAT DO YOU THINK YOU NEED TO #DoBetter ON PURPOSE TOMORROW?

MIND DUMP, PROCESS & UNRAVEL

If you have Accountability **YOU HAVE OWNERSHIP!**

MY DAILY NEWSLETTER
SELF REFLECTION = SELF AWARENESS

WHAT'S 1 THING IN THE *OUTSIDE* WORLD THAT AFFECTED ME TODAY?

WHAT ARE 1-2 THINGS I AM CONTENT WITH IN MY LIFE TODAY? THANKFUL? GRATEFUL?

WHAT 3 THINGS WENT ON TODAY IN *MY WORLD* THAT STOOD OUT? WHAT MADE AN IMPACT?

_____   _____   _____

WHAT DIDN'T GO WELL TODAY?

_____
_____
_____
_____

HOW DID I FEEL EMOTIONALLY? WRITE THEM OUT

− ▬▬▬▬▬▬▬▬ +

_____
_____
_____
_____

HOW DID YOU FEEL PHYSICALLY? WHAT DO I NEED TO ADDRESS?
RESTRICTED BREATHING? ANXIOUSNESS? TENSION? GUT ISSUES? CHEST/BODY PAINS? WITHDRAWN?

_____

ON THE OTHER HAND, WHAT DID GO WELL TODAY?

_____
_____
_____
_____
_____

WHAT CONTRIBUTED TO THINGS GOING WELL?

_____
_____
_____
_____
_____

READ WHAT YOU WROTE ABOVE…WHAT DO YOU THINK YOU NEED TO #DoBetter ON PURPOSE TOMORROW?

_____
_____

MIND DUMP, PROCESS & UNRAVEL

If you have Accountability **YOU HAVE OWNERSHIP!**

MY DAILY NEWSLETTER
SELF REFLECTION = SELF AWARENESS

WHAT'S 1 THING IN THE *OUTSIDE* WORLD THAT AFFECTED ME TODAY?

WHAT ARE 1-2 THINGS I AM CONTENT WITH IN MY LIFE TODAY? THANKFUL? GRATEFUL?

WHAT 3 THINGS WENT ON TODAY IN *MY WORLD* THAT STOOD OUT? WHAT MADE AN IMPACT?

_____   _____   _____

WHAT DIDN'T GO WELL TODAY?

HOW DID I FEEL EMOTIONALLY? WRITE THEM OUT

HOW DID YOU FEEL PHYSICALLY? WHAT DO I NEED TO ADDRESS?
RESTRICTED BREATHING? ANXIOUSNESS? TENSION? GUT ISSUES? CHEST/BODY PAINS? WITHDRAWN?

ON THE OTHER HAND, WHAT DID GO WELL TODAY?

WHAT CONTRIBUTED TO THINGS GOING WELL?

READ WHAT YOU WROTE ABOVE…WHAT DO YOU THINK YOU NEED TO #DoBetter ON PURPOSE TOMORROW?

MIND DUMP, PROCESS & UNRAVEL

If you have Accountability **YOU HAVE OWNERSHIP!**

MY DAILY NEWSLETTER
SELF REFLECTION = SELF AWARENESS

WHAT'S 1 THING IN THE *OUTSIDE* WORLD THAT AFFECTED ME TODAY?

WHAT ARE 1-2 THINGS I AM CONTENT WITH IN MY LIFE TODAY? THANKFUL? GRATEFUL?

WHAT 3 THINGS WENT ON TODAY IN *MY WORLD* THAT STOOD OUT? WHAT MADE AN IMPACT?

WHAT DIDN'T GO WELL TODAY?

HOW DID I FEEL EMOTIONALLY? WRITE THEM OUT

HOW DID YOU FEEL PHYSICALLY? WHAT DO I NEED TO ADDRESS?
RESTRICTED BREATHING? ANXIOUSNESS? TENSION? GUT ISSUES? CHEST/BODY PAINS? WITHDRAWN?

ON THE OTHER HAND, WHAT DID GO WELL TODAY?

WHAT CONTRIBUTED TO THINGS GOING WELL?

READ WHAT YOU WROTE ABOVE... WHAT DO YOU THINK YOU NEED TO #DoBetter ON PURPOSE TOMORROW?

MIND DUMP, PROCESS & UNRAVEL

If you have Accountability **YOU HAVE OWNERSHIP!**

MY DAILY NEWSLETTER
SELF REFLECTION = SELF AWARENESS

WHAT'S 1 THING IN THE *OUTSIDE* WORLD THAT AFFECTED ME TODAY?

WHAT ARE 1-2 THINGS I AM CONTENT WITH IN MY LIFE TODAY? THANKFUL? GRATEFUL?

WHAT 3 THINGS WENT ON TODAY IN *MY WORLD* THAT STOOD OUT? WHAT MADE AN IMPACT?

WHAT DIDN'T GO WELL TODAY?

HOW DID I FEEL EMOTIONALLY? WRITE THEM OUT

HOW DID YOU FEEL PHYSICALLY? WHAT DO I NEED TO ADDRESS?
RESTRICTED BREATHING? ANXIOUSNESS? TENSION? GUT ISSUES? CHEST/BODY PAINS? WITHDRAWN?

ON THE OTHER HAND, WHAT DID GO WELL TODAY?

WHAT CONTRIBUTED TO THINGS GOING WELL?

READ WHAT YOU WROTE ABOVE...WHAT DO YOU THINK YOU NEED TO #DoBetter ON PURPOSE TOMORROW?

MIND DUMP, PROCESS & UNRAVEL

If you have Accountability **YOU HAVE OWNERSHIP!**

MY DAILY NEWSLETTER
SELF REFLECTION = SELF AWARENESS

WHAT'S 1 THING IN THE *OUTSIDE* WORLD THAT AFFECTED ME TODAY?

WHAT ARE 1-2 THINGS I AM CONTENT WITH IN MY LIFE TODAY? THANKFUL? GRATEFUL?

WHAT 3 THINGS WENT ON TODAY IN *MY WORLD* THAT STOOD OUT? WHAT MADE AN IMPACT?

WHAT DIDN'T GO WELL TODAY?

HOW DID I FEEL EMOTIONALLY? WRITE THEM OUT

HOW DID YOU FEEL PHYSICALLY? WHAT DO I NEED TO ADDRESS?
RESTRICTED BREATHING? ANXIOUSNESS? TENSION? GUT ISSUES? CHEST/BODY PAINS? WITHDRAWN?

ON THE OTHER HAND, WHAT DID GO WELL TODAY?

WHAT CONTRIBUTED TO THINGS GOING WELL?

READ WHAT YOU WROTE ABOVE... WHAT DO YOU THINK YOU NEED TO #DoBetter ON PURPOSE TOMORROW?

MIND DUMP, PROCESS & UNRAVEL

If you have Accountability **YOU HAVE OWNERSHIP!**

MY DAILY NEWSLETTER
SELF REFLECTION = SELF AWARENESS

What's 1 thing in the *OUTSIDE* world that Affected me today?

What are 1-2 things I am content with in my life today? Thankful? Grateful?

What 3 things went on today in *My world* that stood out? What made an impact?

_____   _____   _____

What didn't go well today?

_____
_____
_____
_____

How did I feel emotionally? Write them out

– _____ +

_____
_____
_____

How did you feel physically? What do I need to address?
Restricted Breathing? Anxiousness? Tension? Gut issues? Chest/Body Pains? Withdrawn?

_____

On the other hand, What did go well today?

_____
_____
_____
_____
_____

What contributed to things going well?

_____
_____
_____
_____
_____

Read what you wrote above…What do you think you need to #DoBetter on Purpose Tomorrow?

_____
_____

MIND DUMP, PROCESS & UNRAVEL

If you have Accountability **YOU HAVE OWNERSHIP!**

MY DAILY NEWSLETTER
SELF REFLECTION = SELF AWARENESS

What's 1 thing in the *OUTSIDE* world that Affected me today?

What are 1-2 things I am content with in my life today? Thankful? Grateful?

What 3 things went on today in *My world* that stood out? What made an impact?

What didn't go well today?

How did I feel emotionally? Write them out

How did you feel physically? What do I need to address? Restricted Breathing? Anxiousness? Tension? Gut issues? Chest/Body Pains? Withdrawn?

On the other hand, What did go well today?

What contributed to things going well?

Read what you wrote above… What do you think you need to #DoBetter on Purpose Tomorrow?

MIND DUMP, PROCESS & UNRAVEL

If you have Accountability **YOU HAVE OWNERSHIP!**

MY DAILY NEWSLETTER
SELF REFLECTION = SELF AWARENESS

What's 1 thing in the *OUTSIDE* world that Affected me today?

What are 1-2 things I am content with in my life today? Thankful? Grateful?

What 3 things went on today in *My world* that stood out? What made an impact?

_____ _____ _____

What didn't go well today?

_____
_____
_____
_____

How did I feel emotionally? Write them out

– ▬▬▬▬▬▬▬▬▬▬ +

_____
_____
_____

How did you feel physically? What do I need to address?
Restricted Breathing? Anxiousness? Tension? Gut issues? Chest/Body Pains? Withdrawn?

_____

On the other hand, What did go well today?

_____
_____
_____
_____
_____

What contributed to things going well?

_____
_____
_____
_____
_____

Read what you wrote above…What do you think you need to #DoBetter on Purpose Tomorrow?

_____
_____

MIND DUMP, PROCESS & UNRAVEL

If you have Accountability **YOU HAVE OWNERSHIP!**

MY DAILY NEWSLETTER
SELF REFLECTION = SELF AWARENESS

WHAT'S 1 THING IN THE *OUTSIDE* WORLD THAT AFFECTED ME TODAY?

WHAT ARE 1-2 THINGS I AM CONTENT WITH IN MY LIFE TODAY? THANKFUL? GRATEFUL?

WHAT 3 THINGS WENT ON TODAY IN *MY WORLD* THAT STOOD OUT? WHAT MADE AN IMPACT?

WHAT DIDN'T GO WELL TODAY?

HOW DID I FEEL EMOTIONALLY? WRITE THEM OUT

HOW DID YOU FEEL PHYSICALLY? WHAT DO I NEED TO ADDRESS?
RESTRICTED BREATHING? ANXIOUSNESS? TENSION? GUT ISSUES? CHEST/BODY PAINS? WITHDRAWN?

ON THE OTHER HAND, WHAT DID GO WELL TODAY?

WHAT CONTRIBUTED TO THINGS GOING WELL?

READ WHAT YOU WROTE ABOVE...WHAT DO YOU THINK YOU NEED TO #DoBetter ON PURPOSE TOMORROW?

MIND DUMP, PROCESS & UNRAVEL

If you have Accountability **YOU HAVE OWNERSHIP!**

MY DAILY NEWSLETTER
SELF REFLECTION = SELF AWARENESS

WHAT'S 1 THING IN THE *OUTSIDE* WORLD THAT AFFECTED ME TODAY?

WHAT ARE 1-2 THINGS I AM CONTENT WITH IN MY LIFE TODAY? THANKFUL? GRATEFUL?

WHAT 3 THINGS WENT ON TODAY IN *MY WORLD* THAT STOOD OUT? WHAT MADE AN IMPACT?

WHAT DIDN'T GO WELL TODAY?

HOW DID I FEEL EMOTIONALLY? WRITE THEM OUT

HOW DID YOU FEEL PHYSICALLY? WHAT DO I NEED TO ADDRESS?
RESTRICTED BREATHING? ANXIOUSNESS? TENSION? GUT ISSUES? CHEST/BODY PAINS? WITHDRAWN?

ON THE OTHER HAND, WHAT DID GO WELL TODAY?

WHAT CONTRIBUTED TO THINGS GOING WELL?

READ WHAT YOU WROTE ABOVE...WHAT DO YOU THINK YOU NEED TO #DoBetter ON PURPOSE TOMORROW?

MIND DUMP, PROCESS & UNRAVEL

If you have Accountability **YOU HAVE OWNERSHIP!**

MY DAILY NEWSLETTER
SELF REFLECTION = SELF AWARENESS

WHAT'S 1 THING IN THE *OUTSIDE* WORLD THAT AFFECTED ME TODAY?

WHAT ARE 1-2 THINGS I AM CONTENT WITH IN MY LIFE TODAY? THANKFUL? GRATEFUL?

WHAT 3 THINGS WENT ON TODAY IN *MY WORLD* THAT STOOD OUT? WHAT MADE AN IMPACT?

WHAT DIDN'T GO WELL TODAY?

HOW DID I FEEL EMOTIONALLY? WRITE THEM OUT

HOW DID YOU FEEL PHYSICALLY? WHAT DO I NEED TO ADDRESS?
RESTRICTED BREATHING? ANXIOUSNESS? TENSION? GUT ISSUES? CHEST/BODY PAINS? WITHDRAWN?

ON THE OTHER HAND, WHAT DID GO WELL TODAY?

WHAT CONTRIBUTED TO THINGS GOING WELL?

READ WHAT YOU WROTE ABOVE… WHAT DO YOU THINK YOU NEED TO #DoBetter ON PURPOSE TOMORROW?

MIND DUMP, PROCESS & UNRAVEL

If you have Accountability **YOU HAVE OWNERSHIP!**

MY DAILY NEWSLETTER
SELF REFLECTION = SELF AWARENESS

WHAT'S 1 THING IN THE *OUTSIDE* WORLD THAT AFFECTED ME TODAY?
_____

WHAT ARE 1-2 THINGS I AM CONTENT WITH IN MY LIFE TODAY? THANKFUL? GRATEFUL?

WHAT 3 THINGS WENT ON TODAY IN *MY WORLD* THAT STOOD OUT? WHAT MADE AN IMPACT?
_____   _____   _____

WHAT DIDN'T GO WELL TODAY?
_____
_____
_____
_____
_____

HOW DID I FEEL EMOTIONALLY? WRITE THEM OUT
– _____ +
_____
_____
_____

HOW DID YOU FEEL PHYSICALLY? WHAT DO I NEED TO ADDRESS?
RESTRICTED BREATHING? ANXIOUSNESS? TENSION? GUT ISSUES? CHEST/BODY PAINS? WITHDRAWN?
_____

ON THE OTHER HAND, WHAT DID GO WELL TODAY?
_____
_____
_____
_____
_____

WHAT CONTRIBUTED TO THINGS GOING WELL?
_____
_____
_____
_____
_____

READ WHAT YOU WROTE ABOVE...WHAT DO YOU THINK YOU NEED TO #DOBETTER ON PURPOSE TOMORROW?
_____
_____

MIND DUMP, PROCESS & UNRAVEL

If you have Accountability **YOU HAVE OWNERSHIP!**

MY DAILY NEWSLETTER
SELF REFLECTION = SELF AWARENESS

What's 1 thing in the *OUTSIDE* world that Affected me today?

What are 1-2 things I am content with in my life today? Thankful? Grateful?

What 3 things went on today in *My world* that stood out? What made an impact?

What didn't go well today?

How did I feel emotionally? Write them out

How did you feel physically? What do I need to address?
Restricted Breathing? Anxiousness? Tension? Gut issues? Chest/Body Pains? Withdrawn?

On the other hand, What did go well today?

What contributed to things going well?

Read what you wrote above... What do you think you need to #DoBetter on Purpose Tomorrow?

MIND DUMP, PROCESS & UNRAVEL

If you have Accountability **YOU HAVE OWNERSHIP!**

MY DAILY NEWSLETTER
SELF REFLECTION = SELF AWARENESS

WHAT'S 1 THING IN THE *OUTSIDE* WORLD THAT AFFECTED ME TODAY?

WHAT ARE 1-2 THINGS I AM CONTENT WITH IN MY LIFE TODAY? THANKFUL? GRATEFUL?

WHAT 3 THINGS WENT ON TODAY IN *MY WORLD* THAT STOOD OUT? WHAT MADE AN IMPACT?

WHAT DIDN'T GO WELL TODAY?

HOW DID I FEEL EMOTIONALLY? WRITE THEM OUT

HOW DID YOU FEEL PHYSICALLY? WHAT DO I NEED TO ADDRESS?
RESTRICTED BREATHING? ANXIOUSNESS? TENSION? GUT ISSUES? CHEST/BODY PAINS? WITHDRAWN?

ON THE OTHER HAND, WHAT DID GO WELL TODAY?

WHAT CONTRIBUTED TO THINGS GOING WELL?

READ WHAT YOU WROTE ABOVE...WHAT DO YOU THINK YOU NEED TO #DOBETTER ON PURPOSE TOMORROW?

MIND DUMP, PROCESS & UNRAVEL

If you have Accountability **YOU HAVE OWNERSHIP!**

MY DAILY NEWSLETTER
SELF REFLECTION = SELF AWARENESS

WHAT'S 1 THING IN THE *OUTSIDE* WORLD THAT AFFECTED ME TODAY?

WHAT ARE 1-2 THINGS I AM CONTENT WITH IN MY LIFE TODAY? THANKFUL? GRATEFUL?

WHAT 3 THINGS WENT ON TODAY IN *MY WORLD* THAT STOOD OUT? WHAT MADE AN IMPACT?

WHAT DIDN'T GO WELL TODAY?

HOW DID I FEEL EMOTIONALLY? WRITE THEM OUT

HOW DID YOU FEEL PHYSICALLY? WHAT DO I NEED TO ADDRESS?
RESTRICTED BREATHING? ANXIOUSNESS? TENSION? GUT ISSUES? CHEST/BODY PAINS? WITHDRAWN?

ON THE OTHER HAND, WHAT DID GO WELL TODAY?

WHAT CONTRIBUTED TO THINGS GOING WELL?

READ WHAT YOU WROTE ABOVE... WHAT DO YOU THINK YOU NEED TO #DoBetter ON PURPOSE TOMORROW?

MIND DUMP, PROCESS & UNRAVEL

If you have Accountability **YOU HAVE OWNERSHIP!**

MY DAILY NEWSLETTER
SELF REFLECTION = SELF AWARENESS

What's 1 thing in the *OUTSIDE* world that Affected me today?

What are 1-2 things I am content with in my life today? Thankful? Grateful?

What 3 things went on today in *My world* that stood out? What made an impact?

_____   _____   _____

What didn't go well today?

_____
_____
_____
_____

How did I feel emotionally? Write them out

_____
_____
_____

How did you feel physically? What do I need to address? Restricted Breathing? Anxiousness? Tension? Gut issues? Chest/Body Pains? Withdrawn?

_____

On the other hand, What did go well today?

_____
_____
_____
_____
_____

What contributed to things going well?

_____
_____
_____
_____
_____

Read what you wrote above...What do you think you need to #DoBetter on Purpose Tomorrow?

_____
_____

MIND DUMP, PROCESS & UNRAVEL

If you have Accountability **YOU HAVE OWNERSHIP!**

MY DAILY NEWSLETTER
SELF REFLECTION = SELF AWARENESS

WHAT'S 1 THING IN THE *OUTSIDE* WORLD THAT AFFECTED ME TODAY?

WHAT ARE 1-2 THINGS I AM CONTENT WITH IN MY LIFE TODAY? THANKFUL? GRATEFUL?

WHAT 3 THINGS WENT ON TODAY IN *MY WORLD* THAT STOOD OUT? WHAT MADE AN IMPACT?

WHAT DIDN'T GO WELL TODAY?

HOW DID I FEEL EMOTIONALLY? WRITE THEM OUT

HOW DID YOU FEEL PHYSICALLY? WHAT DO I NEED TO ADDRESS?
RESTRICTED BREATHING? ANXIOUSNESS? TENSION? GUT ISSUES? CHEST/BODY PAINS? WITHDRAWN?

ON THE OTHER HAND, WHAT DID GO WELL TODAY?

WHAT CONTRIBUTED TO THINGS GOING WELL?

READ WHAT YOU WROTE ABOVE… WHAT DO YOU THINK YOU NEED TO #DoBetter ON PURPOSE TOMORROW?

MIND DUMP, PROCESS & UNRAVEL

If you have Accountability **YOU HAVE OWNERSHIP!**

MY DAILY NEWSLETTER
SELF REFLECTION = SELF AWARENESS

What's 1 thing in the *OUTSIDE* world that Affected me today?
_____

What are 1-2 things I am content with in my life today? Thankful? Grateful?

What 3 things went on today in *MY WORLD* that stood out? What made an impact?

_____   _____   _____

What didn't go well today?
_____
_____
_____
_____
_____

How did I feel emotionally? Write them out

😞 😟 😐 🙂 😊

—▬▬▬▬▬▬▬▬▬▬▬+

_____
_____
_____

How did you feel physically? What do I need to address?
Restricted Breathing? Anxiousness? Tension? Gut issues? Chest/Body Pains? Withdrawn?
_____

On the other hand, What did go well today?
_____
_____
_____
_____
_____

What contributed to things going well?
_____
_____
_____
_____
_____

Read what you wrote above... What do you think you need to #DoBetter on Purpose Tomorrow?
_____
_____

MIND DUMP, PROCESS & UNRAVEL

Continue the Journey

Pick up another journal from Amazon today!

Let's Stay Connected

@ONPURPOSEPLANNINGANDCONSULTING

FACEBOOK YOUTUBE INSTAGRAM

#DoBetter On Purpose

Made in the USA
Monee, IL
04 February 2023